The essays in I consider pair knowing the self.  writers won't. As relentless as the competitive fencer he is, he thrusts into the dark corners of the ego and the soul, until finally, like all good essayists, he strikes the light, and we, his willing companions stand exposed and grateful in its illumination. Always on the attack, these essays are smart and necessary.

Lee Martin, author of *The Mutual UFO Network*

Kissing the Lobster is a compelling meditation on pain and passion, courage and character, and the inescapable creative urge. Peter Grandbois writes with searing, unflinching honesty. His crisp prose lunges, then drills you directly in the chest.

Dinty W. Moore, author of *Between Panic & Desire*

Self-awareness may be somewhat of a curse for the writer: "Sometimes I fear my entire life is made up of worrying about myself and pretending I'm not." Grandbois writes. This self-awareness might be unpleasant for him but for the reader, it is pure joy. To see Grandbois as he en gardes and touchés as a middle aged man, cracking his own body against his dream of his youth, is to feel what it's like to be a self-aware human—suffering, full of doubt, pointed, sharp, and funny as a sword.

Nicole Walker, author of *Sustainability: A Love Story*

Kissing the Lobster

Peter Grandbois

SPUYTEN DUYVIL
New York City

© 2018 Peter Grandbois
ISBN 978-1-947980-52-5

Library of Congress Cataloging-in-Publication Data

Names: Grandbois, Peter, author.
Title: Kissing the lobster / Peter Grandbois.
Description: New York City : Spuyten Duyvil, [2018]
Identifiers: LCCN 2018014051 | ISBN 9781947980525
Subjects: LCSH: Grandbois, Peter. | Authors, American--21st
    century--Biography.
Classification: LCC PS3607.R3626 Z46 2018 | DDC 813/.6--dc23
LC record available at https://lccn.loc.gov/2018014051

for Tanya

To be nobody-but-yourself—in a world which is doing its best, night and day, to make you everybody else—means to fight the hardest battle which any human being can fight; and never stop fighting.

e.e. cummings

The fencing master does not sell himself. That's his tragedy, and that is also his strength and his glory.

Arturo Perez Reverte

Contents

Bout One:
Pain

It's my destiny to be the king of pain . . .
The Police

The problem with pain is that it's subjective. I could tell you how after fencing in my first North American Cup in seventeen years, I had to stretch for a half hour in my hotel room before I could even walk; how when I did walk, the arthritis in my foot felt like a thousand stinging needles; how when I got to my car, I couldn't lift my legs to get inside, so I had to back in slowly, sitting first on the seat, then trying to swing my legs around, but I couldn't do it because of the sciatica in my back and the pain in my hip, which shot down my leg like fire; how when I tried to lift my legs to tuck them in the car the tendinitis in my right wrist screamed for me to stop, so in the end I had to inch in slowly, clenching my teeth as I swung my legs around.

But it wouldn't mean that much to you. The only real pain is your own.

1969. Age 5.

Your brother throws a Tinker Toy can at you the day after Christmas. The gash on the ridge of your nose streams blood down your face and onto the shag carpet. At the hospital, you watch the needle thread the skin between your eyes, too young to put words to your pain.

1970. Age 6.

You're lying on the orange couch in the living room watching *Star Trek* on the black-and-white console TV, though it doesn't really matter what you're watching because the pneumonia has given you a 103 fever that distorts everything until Kirk blends into Spock, McCoy becomes Scotty, and you're as crazy as Sulu with the "Naked Time" virus. Glistening with sweat, he runs through the upper decks of the *Enterprise*, foil in hand, while you shiver and shake on that old orange couch in your fever-drenched body, your own seemingly disembodied hand rising to summon your mother.

1974. Age 10.

You wake and run to the bathroom, overcome with vomiting and diahrrea. Within twenty-four hours, you're dangerously dehydrated. Your parents take you to the hospital, where you spend the next eight days with your intestines knotted. You lose fifteen pounds—and you were already a skinny kid. The doctors perform test after test but seem to have no idea what's wrong. At one point, they overdose you, and you spend the night hallucinating, positive the nurse is a gorilla trying to keep you trapped in a maze. You hit her when she tries to calm you down. They finally label the mysterious illness "colitis," though they don't sound convinced.

Strangely, there is no pain in these memories. It's almost as if the mind wants to protect you. Yes, you remember feeling humiliated sitting on the toilet with simultaneous vomiting and diahrrea, but you don't remember the actual feeling of humiliation. Yes, you remember that you felt terror at being trapped in that maze, facing the gorilla nurse, but you don't remember what that actual terror felt like, and you have no memory at all of the actual twisting and torqueing of your insides during that week in the hospital when you couldn't keep anything down.

1973. Age 9.

Your father is laid off from his job selling ink, and your mother goes back to work. But that doesn't stop your parents from fighting. Your father even moves out of the house for two weeks, threatening divorce. Your mother, who carried the pain of the death of a sister at age four and of her own father when she was five takes you aside and tells you that you're the man of the house now. You need to be responsible. You nod your head yes and feel the first knot twist your stomach.

Eventually, your father returns—only to threaten to leave many times more over the next decade. Of course, you fulfill your nine-year-old promise.

Within a few months, your parents start a temporary-staffing business together, and you take on the responsibility of caring for your eight-year-old brother and seven-year-old sister after school and throughout the long summer days. Soon you develop pain in your groin. It starts slowly, a slight pull when you walk too fast. Later, it becomes a dull ache any time your legs rub against your scrotum. You touch yourself down there and notice you have what seems like an extra testicle but is really just a herniated muscle. Despite the fact that touching it brings a pain not much different from being kicked in the groin, you can't help but obsessively check it. It's not the first time you have needled at an injured spot on your body in an attempt to understand the pain. It's just the worst time.

Your mom tells you not to worry. She says the surgery for the hernia will be like going to the zoo.

It isn't like going to the zoo.

Is it a coincidence that a year later you develop colitis, a disease linked to nervous system imbalance? No. You've been on that road for quite awhile.

Throughout your childhood, you will get pneumonia twice and strep so many times it will be difficult to imagine yourself without it; and always, since that day in 1973, the knot of anxiety twisting your stomach. Flash forward.

1999. Age 35.

You yearn to be an artist, to create art, to devote yourself entirely to your writing, to the theater, to collaborate with other artists, to write morning, noon, and night, to share your work with others who share the same passion, to write with another, to work with others, to read poetry until two in the morning then talk about it with someone until six, to start your own theater company, to discuss how to bring a work to life on the stage, to share what it means to drop the veil, to open to another's pain, to share your pain with another.

But you are a father, a husband, a businessman. And until now, all you thought you wanted was to play with your children, to take your wife out dancing and make love after, to dress up with your kids for Halloween, to decorate the house for Christmas, take your kids camping, go on family car trips in the summer, play Monopoly and Clue, watch *Star Trek* and old movies as you pass the popcorn, your wife and three kids squished onto the same couch with you, your dogs at your feet. That's all you ever want, until you don't.

Until the day you start writing, February 1st, 1999. Until the morning you wake at 5 a.m. a month and a half after your first child was born and go into the guest bedroom and sit down at the computer and begin to write.

You haven't had a moment of peace since.

1976. Age 12.

Your friend passes you the ball in a backyard basketball game. It hits your left pinky wrong. Jams it into its own socket. Your parents don't believe that it's broken, and so you wait a week before you finally convince them to take you to the doctor. Now they have to re-break it before they can set it again. Your father turns away at the sound.

1985. Age 21.

You're lying in bed after the tonsillectomy, terrified of sleeping, sure you'll drown in the blood that slowly pools in the back of your throat. The pain is unbearable. Nothing like the way they described it in *The Brady Bunch* when Cindy got to eat ice cream all day. There's a lake of fire in the back of your throat. That's how you think of it. It's Lake Erie, 1969, all over again, and you're flailing about in the middle of it, simultaneously drowning and burning.

1986. Age 22.

Back-pedaling from a flèche attack from one of your teammates, you trip over another fencer and break the sesamoid bone in your left foot. Not particularly painful at first, not until you wake the next morning and your foot has swollen to the size of a watermelon. The throbbing sends waves throughout your entire body, making it difficult to concentrate on anything. You have to wear a special shoe for three months.

One day, while walking to class at the University of Colorado, you step on a rock and twist your foot, putting extra pressure on that little broken bone. Maybe the worst pain you've ever felt in your life. You still wince as you remember it thirty years later.

Twenties.

Your twenties are your prime fencing years. Each day you count the yellow bruises and red welts on your chest in the mirror. Sometimes you catch yourself pressing on them while in class or at work just to feel the sharp sting all the way through the bone, as if the pain carried more with it, and if you just kept poking at it, prodding it, you might find the answer to who you really are.

You sprain your ankle seriously at least a half-dozen times during those years, probably many more. And you develop tendinitis in your elbow and hand. You take Advil religiously and tape your hand and wrist before every fencing practice or competition for four years during the high point of your career, from 1991 to 1995. You aren't the only one doing this.

The church of Advil has many disciples. The competition counting welts and bruises after practice is almost as fierce as the fencing. The more tape you use before practice, the more serious you are as an athlete. The more ice after, the more dedicated. These are the rules of your order.

1993. Age 29.

You're fencing for the gold medal in team men's foil at the U.S. Olympic Festival in San Antonio, Texas. There are several hundred people in the audience—not bad for fencing—and your opponent charges, whipping his blade in circles like a blender. You lunge straight into it, hoping to disengage around his blade and let him impale himself. Instead, your blade gets caught up in his. Your arm twists. Your hand snaps. Your friend later says he heard the crack of bone all the way up in the stands.

You drop your blade and cup your hand. You can feel the bones jutting out and you push them back together out of instinct. The room goes wavy as you almost faint. This pain is different from the time you broke your foot. It's not a throb but a surge. Not a wave, but a tsunami that floods your senses so you can't think at all. You sit on the side of the strip. The ref asks if you can still hold the weapon. At first you don't hear him. He asks again. You try but can't move your hand. Game over.

You feel sorry for yourself, for losing the gold, until you arrive at the hospital and sit next to a taekwondo athlete whose face has been kicked in.

1998. Age 34.

The birth of your first child, and the beginning of the deterioration of the discs in your upper back: Maybe it's due to all those years of fencing, the pounding impact of the lunge. Or maybe it's the years that follow. The years when your next two children are born, the years when you'll always seem to be carrying at least one of them on your hip. You'll never really know the cause, though you'll go to every conceivable kind of doctor for years trying to relieve the pain: sports physicians, osteopaths, acupuncturists, physical therapists, and massage therapists. At one point, you'll even think you're starting to fall in love with your masseuse. The removal of pain, even if only temporary, may be the greatest aphrodisiac.

2006. Age 42.

After having completed an MFA and PhD while trying to raise three young children, you take your first professorship, at California State University in Sacramento. And that's when the migraines start—one every month over the next four years, each time knocking you out for a couple days. They always begin the same. Pain moving up your neck and into the back of your head. There's nothing worse than knowing you are about to get a migraine and not being able to do a damn thing about it. Not Advil. Not rest. Not food. Nothing. All you can do is go home and hunker down in bed and hope it won't be one of the bad ones, the kind that hit so hard you throw up. The kind that make sure you don't dare move for three or four days.

Why migraines? You'll never know for sure. But you have a theory. The teaching load is onerous for academia, four classes of thirty to forty students per semester, at that job, plus leading several grad students through their MA theses. Maybe trying to balance writing and work with family (a wife, three children, and a dog) is simply too much. Something has to give.

Maybe this is why the most common pain suffered by people in their thirties is migraines. According to the University at San Francisco Medical School, the peak age for migraines is between thirty-five and forty-five. Interestingly, you'd never suffered migraines before age forty-two, and the migraines stop four years later, when you take a more accommodating job at Denison University in Ohio. Now you don't even know if they were migraines. Doctors say that what some of us call migraines are really tension headaches. All you know is that nothing could get rid of them and that once the pain debilitated you, made it so you couldn't do anything but lie down and cry, you didn't care what they were called. You only wanted them to go away.

The body lets us know when something is off in our lives. But it doesn't always tell us *what* is off.

2012. Age 48.

As you sit in your living room chair typing away on the first draft of this essay, you attempt to turn around to make sure your two German Shepherds haven't tried to eat your new kittens, but you can't turn around because of a kinked neck, something that seems a regular part of life lately. Maybe it's related to the degenerating discs in your back. Maybe it's something new.

So to check on the kittens you have to get out of the chair. The pain begins in your lower back as you try to stand, follows through your hip as you turn, and catches the arthritis in the ball of your left foot as you plant your weight on it. Time to stretch. There is value to pain. We evolved nerve cells for a reason: to tell us when something is wrong, to tell us when to stop doing something.

Not that we always listen. At least you don't, much to your oldest daughter's dismay. She shoots you a look every time you complain about how difficult it is to walk after fencing (yes, you continue to fence) the night before.

We often say something is not worth doing unless it's difficult. And isn't your mantra "No pain, no gain?" That's what your high school football coach drilled into you. As writers we love to talk about how difficult the work is, how much pain it causes us:

"Writing a novel is a terrible experience, during which the hair often falls out and the teeth decay."—Flannery O'Connor

"Writing is easy. You just stare at a blank page until your forehead bleeds." –Attributed to both Gene Fowler and Douglas Adams

"Writing is easy; You just open a vein and bleed."—Often attributed to Red Smith, but also to Ernest Hemingway and Thomas Wolfe

Difficulty is another measure of pain, and we measure

the worth of something, at least in part, by its difficulty.

That's it, isn't it? Difficulty as measured by the mind, by the blood that seeps from our forehead. Pain means nothing without the mind to perceive it. The International Association for the Study of Pain defines pain as "an unpleasant sensory and emotional experience associated with actual or potential tissue damage." In other words, pain doesn't have to be "real," or somatic, to be experienced.

There are several steps to pain perception, which relies on the fact that the brain receives and processes the signal from the nerve cells. But what if the brain receives a faulty signal? After amputation of a limb or breast, ninety to ninety-eight percent of patients report feeling a phantom sensation. Sometimes, these sensations go on for weeks, and in the majority of cases, these sensations are painful.

What possible value is there in imagining pain from a limb that no longer exists? Perhaps we don't want to let go, and the pain is the only reminder we have of that thing to which we dearly wish to hold. When the pain is gone, the thing is gone. In that way, phantom pain is not so rare, not so mysterious. We all have it. We all carry with us the pain of those things of which we refuse to let go.

You dig deeper into pain, deeper into your past.

1995. Age 31.

A year after cheating on your first wife, you marry the woman with whom you were having the affair. And you quit (temporarily) fencing, a sport that was your life for the previous twelve years.

It's taken you a very long time to understand why you quit, just as it will take a very long time to return to the sport, as you've done recently. Seventeen years, in fact. For seventeen years you'll hold on to the guilt you carry over that affair, that divorce. For seventeen years you tell yourself you no longer want to fence, when what you really want is a convenient excuse for the failure of your first marriage. You tell yourself that your obsession over making the Olympic team destroyed that marriage. And you aren't about to let that happen again.

Maybe that's true. Maybe that is the reason you quit fencing. But just maybe there is another a reason, a refusal to let go of the guilt, the pain of that phantom marriage.

Physical pain as the bridge to psychological pain. Physical pain as a coping mechanism for the million different slings and arrows of psychological agony that afflict the body as we grow up. You've heard about teenagers who cut themselves, but you never understood the reason. Not until you witnessed your own teenage daughter cutting her arm over and over with a butcher knife, then rubbing lemon juice in the wounds, all to quiet the even more painful wound brought on by the OCD that tortured her mind. You've heard about tribes that scar themselves to mark the grief of a significant loss, but again, you never really understood until you scarred your own body, inflicting pain on it over and over again by fencing harder than you should, failing to listen to the body's warning to stop—all because you grieved. And what did you grieve? Oh, so many things—the loss of the self you thought you knew, the loss of the family you thought was your solid center, and more, so much more.

It's a small leap from phantom limbs to phantoms of psychological pain. But if we're hesitant talking of our physical pain, we are downright silent about our psychic pain.

If we do talk about it, it's in hushed murmurs behind closed doors. *I'm taking Prozac. Zoloft. Lexapro. Only for a while until I get myself together. Just to get me through a rough patch.*

The rate of antidepressant use in the U.S. increased nearly four hundred percent between 1990 and 2010 according to a report by Janice Wood on PsychCentral.com. The same antidepressants are the third most common prescription drug taken by Americans and the most frequently used by those between the ages of eighteen and forty-four. We may not talk much about it, but we seek out relief by the millions.

Drugs aren't the only way to cover up pain. Work can cover up pain. Sport can cover up pain. Anything we do to excess so we don't have to think, don't have to feel.

Any addiction, in the end, is about covering up pain—even if many of those methods actually bring more pain.

After having trouble keeping up with the latest addictions, such as internet pornography and gambling, the most recent revision of the *Diagnostic and Statistical Manual of Mental Disorders* (the official handbook of the American Psychiatric Association) now includes the catchall phrase of "behavioral addiction" to cover all forms—simply because we, as human beings, are endlessly creative in finding ways to hide our pain.

When you were younger, you hid from your pain by reading. Now you see your second child do the same thing. How can a parent (especially one who reads and writes for a living) tell his child to take a break from reading? How can reading ever be bad? You tell yourself that you returned to fencing at the age of forty-eight because your kids wanted to fence too, but the truth is, you pushed them, just a little.

The truth is, you couldn't sit alone with the knot of anxiety in your stomach. The knot that has been there for as long as you can remember. The knot that has been getting progressively worse over the last couple years. You don't want to know what it's telling you. You don't want to listen. And so you fence again.

2012. Age 48.

The "Turkey Classic" Thanksgiving weekend fencing tournament in Columbus, Ohio, is your first tournament in seventeen years. You've been fencing again for a month. Not enough time. Not when you're nearly fifty. Still, you feel pretty good in your first three bouts. Almost as if you'd never stopped. Then you face a twenty-one-year-old "A"-rated fencer (the highest rating in American fencing, equivalent to a black belt in karate). You have to come out strong, so you chase him down the strip before he can even think of chasing you.

You finish the attack with a ballestra (jump) lunge. A searing fire shoots through your left foot. For a moment, you're sure that it's the sesamoid bone again, but then the pain turns to tingling, and you realize you've simply strained the tendons.

It hurts to walk. It hurts to *move,* but you don't stop. You don't listen to your body. You chase him down again and again, each time limping back to the *en garde* line.

You lose both touches and the bout. Later, in the first bout of the direct elimination, you pull a groin muscle. In the second direct elimination bout, your hip goes out.

You stretch between bouts, telling yourself that you're still in it. That you can finish the tournament. That you can win. Why don't you admit that you've overdone it? Why don't you acknowledge that fencing a tournament with much younger fencers after only a month of training is foolish at best? Why don't you quit before you hurt yourself? Quitting never enters your mind.

When you fence, the knot in your stomach is gone. When you fence, you forget who you are, at least for a little while. You forget who you've been. You forget what you fear, what you yearn for. You exist in that place where time stops. Where there's only the freedom to kill or be killed. The physical pain is simply a reminder that your need for that moment is unhealthy. When you limp back to the car, you feel strangely satisfied, as if part of you wanted the pain.

That's something else we don't talk about: the fact that most of us don't like ourselves all that much. Some of us even hate ourselves, though we'd rarely admit it. But if we are honest, a streak of self-loathing runs deep in most of us. Pain can be a method of managing that self-loathing.

We are not that far from medieval penitents flogging ourselves. Those times we push ourselves harder than we should, knowing we will pay the price, knowing it might not be good for us. Why don't we stop? Why does the mind assert its power, ignoring the body's cries to quit before we are hurt? I don't have an answer yet. I think we wait our whole lives for that answer. I think discovering the honest answer to that question may be the purpose of living lives filled with pain.

2012. Age 48. Looking backward.

It's April. Six months before your return to fencing. Seven months before the tournament where you will want to hurt yourself.

You've moved out of the house. You've been living on your own for the last week. After a year of depression. After another year of questioning who you are and what you want, you moved into a house two doors down from your own.

You watch your son try to hide his pain in uncomfortable laughter as you and your second wife fight in front of him, sometimes violently. You watch your oldest daughter walking circles around the outside of the house whenever both parents are inside, her muscles taut as a doe that knows instinctively something is wrong. You watch your second daughter, your middle child, develop an alternate psychic reality involving aliens who are trying to kidnap her, to do her harm. She's always had a vivid imagination, and now that imagination has turned against her to the point of causing nightly panic attacks.

In short, you are not only repeating the story of your parents' marriage, but revisiting the trauma of that time in 1973 on your own children, a time that for you lasted the next ten years until you were safely ensconced in college, and your parents, for some reason they've never fully been able to explain, stopped fighting.

But you can't do it. After a week, you move back in. You think the pain is over. That you've figured out your decision. Figured out what you want, who you are. But you don't understand it's only the beginning of the pain.

2015. Age 51.

It's been nearly three years of therapy since you moved out of the house, and you still don't have a clue how to stop the war inside, how to balance your identity as a responsible, loving, family man with your identity as a selfish, dedicated artist. You are more than selfish. You have an ego that wants and wants. How to face the fact that you were willing (may be willing still) to abandon one self for the other, one life for another?

Your second wife says it's because you're a writer, that being an artist means you want more than other people, that an essential tenet of being an artist is dissatisfaction with what you have, who you are, how the world works. You want something better, something more. And because you can't have it, there is pain. And so, the knot grows in your stomach even as you write this.

You go to a one-week intensive group therapy session. You call it "Crazy Camp." The name doesn't begin to do it justice. Each morning one counselor and ten patients enter a room no bigger than a small bedroom. You spend eight hours a day in that room, telling each other your pain, helping each other act it out, helping your bodies to work through it. You absorb more psychic pain there than anyone has a right to: people who've been abused, people whose own parents tried to kill them, people who were imprisoned as sex slaves as children. Next to theirs, your own pain seems minuscule, nonexistent. But for some reason, they listen and cry along with you. For some reason, during that short week, you, the counselor, and those ten other patients drop the veil, and reach across that chasm to hold each other's pain.

It's the first time you realize that pain defines who we are, though most of us keep it hidden most of the time. Some days you wonder what might have happened had you not moved back into your house. You use your writer's imagination to project yourself into that life without your wife and children. You imagine sharing your life with those who share your passion. You dream about dropping the veil, about speaking your language and finding those who speak it, too, finding those who share your pain, as if that miracle of "Crazy Camp" could somehow manifest itself in the outside world. They are out there, the people who talk about Rilke as if that's where truth lies.

But, most of the time, you think you would only be living in a different kind of pain. You would fulfill one half of who you are and lose the other. You wonder if this desire for the other life, whatever life it is that we can't have, is at the root of all our psychic pain. We want what we can't have. Or rather, what we want always has a price. The question is: Are you willing to pay it? How to reconcile yourself with yourself? How to face the fact that you're not the person you thought you were?

Nothing begins, and nothing ends,
That is not paid with moan,
For we are born in others' pain,
And perish in our own.

The English poet Francis Thompson wrote those lines in the late nineteenth century. He was an opium addict who died homeless on the street of tuberculosis at age forty-eight.

Some pain is existential. We are born with it. It's the price of being alive. But then there is that other pain. The one we don't want to acknowledge. The pain that is our body's way of telling us something is wrong. The pain that is really the body's way of giving voice to the ghost of past choices that haunts us, that works its way inside us, demanding that we take a long, hard look. When we don't. When we choose to cover it up, when we ignore that pain, it is at our peril. The knot in our stomach becomes an ulcer, becomes cancer, becomes a series of bones broken for no good reason.

We say, *Isn't it sad that he was struck down so early in life. How unfair that his body betrayed him.*

Deep inside, we feel the lie. We know it wasn't his body that betrayed him at all. His body was the only thing screaming to save him.

Bout Two:
Exhaustion

You're tired. But everyone is tired. But no one is tired enough.
Galway Kinnell

July 2013, U.S. National Championships,
Veteran's Division: Age 49

You didn't sleep the night before. Acid reflux. It sounds silly, but you'd never felt so miserable. You were sure you weren't going to fence the next morning. You rose from bed, positive you weren't going to fence. Except you did. Now it's the middle of the day and you're facing your second direct elimination bout. You wonder what you're doing here without breakfast, without sleep. The Columbus convention center must hold two thousand fencers this morning, though twelve thousand will move in and out of its halls throughout the week. They run back and forth, carrying their equipment, searching the large hall for their strip assignment. The clank of steel punctuated by screams already fills the air. You sit strip side in those uncomfortable convention center chairs, a towel wrapped around your neck, yours sweats covering your legs.

The referee calls you to *en-garde*. Your opponent is balding, with a bit of a belly. He doesn't look like he can move fast. Good, you think. Maybe this will be easy. Until you remember, you are old, too.

7am

Wake up. Wake the kids up. Brush your teeth. Brush their teeth. Shower. Make sure the kids shower. Get dressed. Set out your son's clothes. Brush your hair. Wet down that cowlick on your son's head. Comb your daughter's bangs back. Feed dogs. Feed kids. Give dogs water. Give kids juice. Put collars on dogs. Put collars on . . . no! Make sure kids feed cats. Make toast to eat. Keep dogs from stealing cats' food. Keep kids from stealing toast. Take pill for acid reflux. Sprinkle son's medicine in his juice. Remind yourself to eat. Tell second daughter she needs to eat or she won't be going to school. Remind yourself of the day's schedule. Remind the kids of the day's schedule. Remind kids to clean the dishes. Take empty cereal boxes back with you to the kitchen to throw away. Empty out dishwasher. Tell kids to empty out lunch boxes from the day before. Make kids' lunches: peanut butter and jelly, applesauce, Cheez-its, yogurt, and a snack bar. Pack kids' lunches in backpacks. Remind son to brush his teeth because he didn't do it the first time. Remind yourself to make more toast as the toast you made is gone. Tell oldest daughter to wear a coat because it's ten degrees out. Tell son to re-comb his hair while you're gone because the cowlick is standing again. Tell oldest daughter to put her coat on again. Make toast for middle child because she still hasn't eaten. Carry toast to the car for her to be sure she eats. Drive daughters to school. Hug daughters goodbye. Drive back home. Pick up son and drive him to the bus stop. Wait with son for bus. Give son hug. Drive home. Let dogs out. Let cats out. Do breakfast dishes. Feed fish. Remind yourself to eat.

You've never been able to adjust to fencing in the older division, so at the command to fence, you bounce around like the fighter you used to be. Moving in and out, changing tempo, shifting the size of your steps, waiting for the right moment. There it is. You make a beat lunge, but his hand is quick. He parries your attack and sends his riposte. 1-0 against you. The same thing happens the second time and the third. Now you're down 3-0, and suddenly it's getting more difficult to bounce. You can't rely on the speed you no longer have. You'll have to set up the attack. Use second intention. Give a false attack, let him think he has the parry, then hit him hard with your own counter parry riposte. It works. You take your time. Work your way back to 3-3. The only problem is that setting up your attack takes more energy, and your legs are already wobbly.

8am

Blank page. Blank page. Blank page. Write a word. A phrase. A sentence. Delete it. Blank page. Blank page. Blank page. Try again. Yes. The phrase is good. Yes. Yes. Maybe. No. It's wrong. Delete it. Blank page. All you're doing is complaining. Writing down your complaints. This is not writing. So, you stare out the window and watch the leaves fall. Listen to your dog bark to be let inside. Let your dog inside. Sit and think. What is it you need to write? What is it you need to say? The dog barks to be let out. Let the dog out. That's it! You've got it. Sit down to write. Write that one true sentence. No. It's wrong. Delete it. Blank page. Blank page. Blank page. How much have you written so far? Nothing. Two hours wasted. A day wasted. The thought is too much to bear. The thought is enough to make you curl up in bed and pull the covers over. But you don't. You stick it out. Blank page. Blank page. Blank page. Nothing comes to you. Not a word. Not an idea. It's like trying to give birth, but the baby is stuck at the shoulders. Like trying to shit, but being constipated. It's like pressing your head against a cheese grater, trying to push it through, hoping words come out. The dog barks to come back inside. Get up and let him in. Check your email. Check Facebook. Sit and press your head against the grinder of the Blank page. Blank page. Blank page.

It starts as a burning in your chest, this feeling that you can't breathe. No matter what you do you can't get enough air. Your legs no longer respond. Your mind doesn't understand. Your mind still thinks you're twenty-seven and at your fencing prime. Why won't these legs work? The mind wants to know! Ballestra with second intention. Give an opening in four, then sweep the line with circle four and advance lunge. Except when your body tries to execute the command from your unrelenting mind, the legs simply don't respond, or if they do it's as a parody of the image in your mind. The foil is a dead weight in your hand, like trying to conduct a symphony with a cement block. Your arm simply can't make the intricate motions your mind demands. The muscles aren't getting enough oxygen, and they are rebelling. Breathe, damn it! You recall that scene in Cameron's *The Abyss*, the one where Ed Harris' character puts on the experimental scuba gear that allows him to breathe water. You remember the way his body goes into shock, rebelling against the very idea. Well, that's what your body is doing now. You finally understand the term "sucking air." Only this air is so thick, you couldn't suck it with a straw. You've got to gulp it down in large chunks, but your chest won't take it in.

10am

Sit in your office at Denison and read over your comments on the student pieces you already read twice yesterday. Write down your plan for how to lead the workshop, what questions to ask, what passages to point out. Don't think as you repeat for the ten thousandth time in your ten year college teaching career: "Need balance of scene," "Show don't tell," "Avoid generalizations or abstractions," "Avoid filter statements," "Every detail should be significant," "Every detail should do one, both, or all of the following: move the plot forward, develop character, develop theme," "Every detail should be concrete, specific, and vivid." Be generous in your comments. Find something that is working in every piece. Remember what your writing was like at that age. Be careful not to overwhelm them with criticism. Read the stories you assigned to them in the last class, stories from contemporary masters you read the night before, pieces you already read last semester and the semester before that. Plan how to use those pieces to illuminate the weaknesses in the student writing. If time, write one of the many, many letters of recommendation you need to write, or respond to one of the seemingly infinite number of emails waiting in bold face in your inbox. Too late. Time to teach.

Your opponent attacks. A simple lunge to the chest. You should have been able to move, to get out of the way. The score is even at 5-5. You take off your mask and walk to the end of the strip. Stalling for time, for breath. The ref asks you to get *en-garde*. Just a moment, you reply. If you don't get *en-garde,* I'll have to give you a yellow card, the ref replies. He's not used to refereeing the veteran's competitions, not aware of the fact that if his competitors don't take a break, they might go into cardiac arrest. You put your mask back on and let the ref know you're ready. *Allez!* You're not about to lose this one, especially not because you're out of shape, so you push your opponent down the strip with multiple feint attacks. He takes the bait. Advance lunge! Touché! But now he comes at you strong, and you've used up whatever energy you had left. No matter. There's more, isn't there? You can do this. Push back. It's a dance, each fencer taking his turn to lead the other. Wait for the right moment. Ignore the burn. Wait for the moment to break his rhythm. Ignore the fact that each time you move you feel as if you'll fall. Fake lunge to his flank. He parries eight. You still have instinct, you still have all those years of training. What does it matter if the training was seventeen years ago? You stop on a dime and make a counter-riposte to his belly. You're up 7-5. If only the bout could end now.

12pm

Good afternoon. How's everyone doing? Blank stares. Write the quote for the day on the board. Pass out papers. Take roll. Take a drink of water and run your plan for the lesson through your head one last time. Go over the homework assignment for the next class. Blank stares. Begin workshop by having student read the excerpt you chose from their work. Why does it make sense to start the piece here? Blank stares. Well, what is this piece about? Blank stares. What does this piece want to be about? A meek hand rises. "The story follows two penguins as each tries to get the other to jump off the iceberg and into the water first." Okay, good. That's the literal plot, but what about the subtext? Blank stares. Well, what do the penguins want? A meek hand rises. "They want to get in the water." Okay, good. That is literally what they want, but what do they yearn for? What is at stake for them? Blank stares. Let's look at this line on page three: "As he began to look at the horizon, he was wishing he could be some place else, wishing he could be a different penguin." Forget the filters and bland constructions. Forget the fact that the writer tells us what the penguin wants instead of letting that yearning rise up organically through his actions, and please just tell me what the penguin wants. Blank stares.

There's still a whole minute on the time clock. Anything can happen in a minute of fencing time. You've got to wait him out. You need the minute rest period. But it seems like the last minute revitalized him, and your legs are shouting, "Fuck you! I'm not doing this anymore!" It's okay. Your defense is strong. You've always had a quick hand. Just play the distance. Make him think he's choosing when to attack. Then nail him with a riposte. He's coming strong with a coupe to your six line. Retreat and close six. You stopped him cold. He comes again with a coupe to six, and this time you're sure you've got him. He feints six to trigger your parry. You give it to him. And he disengages to your four line just the way you wanted. Hammer your riposte home. Except you don't. When you make the parry, you don't have the strength to control your point. Your blade glides past his belly without scoring the touch. He hits on a remise. 6-7.

2pm

Grade paper after paper. ""Bangkok" by James Salter is a really interesting story. I really liked "Bangkok."" No matter how many times you tell them it's not a response paper, you still get the same generic openings. Make sure your comments are legible even after grading twenty papers. An impossible task. Try to make each comment sound fresh even though you've said each thousands and thousands of times: "Excellent work! I love your point about…., but push to support your argument with specific quotes," "Nice work! I love your point about….but remember to focus on one aspect of craft and develop how it creates meaning in the work." Read another paper, and another. Keep writing those comments. Don't think. You don't have time. Keep reading. Keep writing. Don't stop to count how many papers you have left. It will only depress you. Twenty-four more. Shit! No time to finish. You've got to prepare your lessons for tomorrow.

He knows you can't move. He sees your dropped guard. He notes your hunched body, the way your back foot drags. He can tell it's only a matter of time. And there's all the time in the world. Forty-five seconds. An eternity in fencing time. He knows you can't sustain a compound attack. You can't coordinate a retreat with an effective defense. So he comes at you. Small steps. Slow at first. Only when he's got you at the end of the strip does he accelerate, beat disengage, one-two. 7-7. Forty seconds on the clock. You tell yourself to stop looking at the time, but you can't help it. Forty seconds until you can breathe again. Forty seconds until you can sit. Forty seconds until your legs stop burning. But you've got pride. Your coach, Henri, worked hard to make sure you understood what pride meant. You don't give up. You don't lose to a fencer who is not as good as you, and despite appearances your opponent is not as good. So you tell yourself you're going to move. You tell yourself it's all or nothing. You tell yourself you'd rather get that final touch, take two steps off the strip and drop dead than lose. *En-garde.* Are you ready?

4pm

Pick up daughter from cross-country practice and take her home. Drive other daughter to orthodontist appointment and come home. Take son to karate class. While he is in karate do grocery shopping for the week. Pick up dry cleaning. Race home to get dinner started. Yell at kids to set the table. Prepare the harp to take daughter to orchestra practice. Yell at kids to set the table again because they didn't do it the first time. Pack harp in the car. Yell at kids to set the table so loudly they think you are going to have an aneurism. They set the table mainly because they are afraid if you die they will have to make dinner, too. Eat dinner. Yell at youngest child to stay seated at the table. Ask each of your kids about their day. Listen as you get detailed descriptions of the dreams they had the night before or the movie their friend saw last night. Yell at youngest child to stay seated at the table again. Tell him if he doesn't finish his food there will be a consequence, though the idea of having to think of a consequence at the moment is too much. You hope he won't call your bluff. Drive oldest daughter to orchestra practice. Grade papers or plan lessons while you wait for her. Drive her home and unpack the harp.

You're focused. You're in the zone. It doesn't matter that your heart feels like it's going to explode. It doesn't matter that you can't ever seem to get enough air. You're moving and that's what counts. You're creating the rhythm. You're dictating the tempo. And now you've got him. Give him the opening. Draw his attack, then circle six coupe to the back. 8-7. Yes. You can do this. *En-garde. Allez!* Keep pushing. Don't let him steal the rhythm. Two more touches and you're there. Two more touches and you're golden. March him down the strip. That's it! You're fencing like you're twenty again. Ballestra lunge. He parries and retreats. You redouble your attack. Beat feint low, then accelerate to the high line. 9-7. You've got it. You're going to win. One more touch and you can rest. There's only one problem. You're pretty sure you're going to throw up.

9pm

Daddy, can you come to the bedroom with me, I'm scared. Daddy, can you read me a book? Daddy, can you get me a glass of water? Daddy, can you make me a toast? Daddy, I forgot to do my homework. Will you help me? Daddy, can you tickle my back? Daddy, can you give me a whisker kiss? Daddy, can you give me a head massage? Daddy, can you tell me a story? Daddy, can you tell me why the world is the way it is? Why people are mean? Why some kids have to be bullies? Why I'm sad? Why my mind tells me horrible things? Why my friends all have cell phones and I don't? Why other parents buy their kids whatever they want? *Jason has an X-box with Skylanders!* Daddy, can you tell me a good dream so I won't have bad dreams? Daddy, can you make my room safe? Daddy, can you shut the closet door so the bogeyman can't get out? Daddy, can you check under the bed? Daddy, can you lie here with me until I fall asleep?

Twenty-two seconds on the clock, and he's coming hard. He pulls his arm back, inviting your counter. You take it because it's easy. You take it because you're going to puke any second. You know the moment you extend your arm that you're done for. He wraps your blade in a sweeping seven parry and hits your flank. 9-8. Okay. Okay. You still have the lead. All you need is one more touch, and time is on your side. Hold him off. All you have to do is stay away from him for 16 seconds. You take off your mask, tell the ref you need to tie your shoe, but he's not buying it. *En-garde!*

10pm

We need to communicate. Talk to me. Do you love me? Do I look good? No, I mean do you really love me? I need time with you. Don't you want to spend time with me? Do you want to have sex? Make love? Screw? I need love. I need a massage. I need you. I need you to watch the kids. I need you to watch TV with me. I need you to dance with me, to go to a movie with me. Let's go for a walk. Let's go for a date night. Let's go visit my mother. Can you help me? Can you get me a glass of water? Can you hold me? Can you handle dinner tonight? Can you handle breakfast? Can you handle lunch? Can you put the kids to bed? Can I tell you a story about a kid at school? This needs to be repaired. This *thing* needs to be repaired! *I* need you to fix this. The sink leaks. The well isn't working. The toilet is plugged. The paint is chipping. The walls are smudged. The carpet is torn. The walls are cracked. The fireplace is cracked. The house is cracked. You are cracked. You need to get fixed. There's something wrong with you. Are you sure you're getting enough Vitamin D?

Fifteen. Fourteen. Thirteen. He's pressing you hard, and you can't seem to keep him away. You tried to attack into his preparation, even to launch a counter attack, but your legs have nothing left. It's all they can do to keep you on your feet. Still, he keeps coming. You're going to have to give him an opening and go for the parry riposte. Defense is all you've got. But even then you have to retreat. Your legs have to move a little. Twelve, Eleven, Ten. He's coming low. Okay, give him the opening in eight. It's one of your favorite parries. It doesn't matter that you can't feel your arm, you can always parry eight. He lunges hard and fast. Your hand moves to eight, but your legs don't retreat, so your hand arrives too late. 9-9.

11pm

Read stories and judge them. Read poems and judge them. Read essays and judge them. All while lying in your bed. You edit for a couple national literary magazines. Read one after the other, then click the "reject" button, sending it back home to whoever wrote it, whoever clearly loved the piece more than you. It amazes you that no matter how badly you feel, the moment you see a story that works, a poem that sings, you are awake. There is nothing better. And that's why you do it. But those moments are few and far between. So, for tonight it's read and reject, read and reject, read and reject until you can't tell the difference between waking and sleep.

Six seconds on the clock. The next touch wins. If the clock runs out, you go into sudden death overtime. You don't want that. More fencing is the last thing you want. You'll throw up in your mask, and that wouldn't be pretty. No. You've got to make it happen. Will your legs to move, your arm to work. *Allez!* He's running straight at you. Retreat. Retreat. Wait for the opening. Five. Four. Three. Two. That's it! You fooled him into attacking too early. He must be tired, too. You've got the right distance. Now parry four and straight riposte to the chest. Nothing fancy. Nothing risky. Just hit him square in the chest. See the point all the way to the target. But your arm is stone. Your point glances his chest, slipping off before the machine can register a touch. He falls into you, jabbing. 10-9 for your opponent. The clock buzzes zero. Time's up. You shake his hand, then walk to the end of the strip. You bend at the waist. Hands on knees, trying to hold yourself up, to brace yourself, sure you will either throw up or keel over.

Midnight

Surrender. Trust in sleep. Trust in the weight of your body. Close your eyes and feel what it's like to sink into your pillow, to fall deeper and deeper into yourself. There's no need for a Venti Latte or Carmel Macchiato. No need for a Coke or a coffee, or a Red Bull. No need for tea, or a Jolt, or Ben and Jerry's Coffee Fudge Ice Cream. No need for dark chocolate, or Pepsi One, or Mountain Dew. You can let go now. You've done your time.

Each minute about five quarts of blood flow through our hearts. Each day our hearts beat about 100,000 times and pump about 1,900 gallons of blood. In a seventy-year lifespan, the average human heart beats more than 2.5 billion times.[1] A person at rest breathes between twelve and fifteen times a minute. That's 17,000 times a day. Over six million breaths a year, half a billion breaths in an average lifetime.[2] But the work ethic of the human brain makes even that Herculean task seem paltry. It's estimated that the brain makes 100 trillion calculations per second.[3] Don't even attempt to extrapolate how many calculations in an average lifetime. The number of zero's would fill several pages. To try to stop the body or even slow it down from its dizzying pace is to deny life. To deny that primitive pulse inside that will not be silenced. Yet, as we age we do slow down. Or at least we would if we didn't keep pushing ourselves. As a culture, we want more. More time. More money. More life. Fucker! And we want it with no strings attached. Ninety percent of Americans consume caffeine in one form or another every single day.[4] We want to work, but we don't want to be tired. We grow old, but we don't want to rest. We fight it anyway we can. And yet.

Exhaustion is life.

I wonder about asking the body to give more than it already does. Exhaustion reminds us to listen. To listen and to know when the body is tired, when the mind needs a rest. There's something akin to denial in the way we use caffeine. It's as if we don't want to admit we're tired because we equate that tiredness with our own mortality. That denial, that detachment from body seems antithetical to life. Death in the sense that we no longer hear what the body requires.

I've fought exhaustion my entire adult life. Telling myself I can do more. I don't need to sleep. Pushing myself to be efficient, looking for ways to double task. *If you're going to the bathroom, empty the trash. If you're heading to the kitchen, collect the dirty glasses on the way.* We forget that simply living is exhausting, moving through this earth with seven billion other people is often more than the body can bear. We forget to forgive ourselves when we collapse on the sofa after a long day, or when we sit in front of the TV with a beer. Instead of surrender to our own exhausting lives, we drink a coffee or soda or pop a pill and say do more.

What might happen if we stopped? Would we die? Sink to the bottom like a shark that stops swimming? Our bodies would certainly be healthier. We say to each other: "I'm so tired. I need to rest," when what we really mean is I want my life to stop for a moment. I want to get off the ride and look around. But we don't say that. In saying "I'm so tired," what we're really saying is "I can't stop. I'm afraid to stop," because of course, it's frightening to stop.

What might happen if you sat down in that chair and did . . . nothing? Do you feel how your body surrenders to the soft cushions, how the cat clawing in your gut settles into a purring ball of fur? Go ahead. You're almost fifty. Relax and look around. Just don't look too closely at yourself. That way madness lies. You have a lifetime of regrets to think about, mistakes and misdirections. Don't listen to the voice whispering in your ear: *Who are you? What are you doing?*

Notes

1. Boston Scientific. Lifebeat. "How Your Heart Works." http://www.bostonscientific.com/lifebeat-online/heart-smart/how-your-heart-works.html (accessed September 10, 2014).

2. American Lung Association. "How Lungs Work." http://www.lung.org/your-lungs/how-lungs-work/?gclid=CN2V79fR5LoC-FUPl7Aod-1cAAg (accessed September 10, 2014).

3. Delio, Michelle. "This is Your Computer on Brains." Wired. http://www.wired.com/techbiz/it/news/2002/11/56459 (accessed September 10, 2014).

4. Villanova University: Student Life. About Caffeine. http://www1.villanova.edu/villanova/studentlife/health/promotion/goto/resources/drugs/caffeine.html (accessed September 10, 2014).

Bout Three: Humility

It ain't the heat, it's the humility.
Yogi Berra

I've often wondered how much time I spend thinking about myself. I mean if you could quantify it, measure it, scientifically scrutinize how many seconds, minutes, hours each day you spend worrying about your problems, thinking about what others think of you, or flat out obsessing over who you are and what you want, what would it add up to? I'm almost afraid to find out. Afraid of what it would say about me. What it would say about us as human beings. I tell myself that I have to google my name regularly to find out if one of my books has been reviewed or won an award. And truth be told, I've discovered quite a few reviews and awards I didn't know about this way. Strange how the writer is often the last to know. I tell myself I need to do this for my CV. Academia is nothing if not obsessed with marking each line item on your CV for tenure. So, I tell myself it's part of my job. But deep down I know better. I know the stench of ego when I smell it.

If I had any humility I would be perfect.—Ted Turner

Many people have told me over the years that I'm one of the most humble people they know. My high school drama teacher even wrote that in my senior yearbook. What does it say about me that I take pride in the fact that people think I'm humble? I go out of my way to appear more humble. I try not to talk about a new book of mine when it comes out. Though I do post an announcement on Facebook. I tell myself it's marketing, that it's the least I can do for my book. Yesterday, I was at a department meeting and the chair congratulated each person who had a new book or article coming out. I had a book just out, and she didn't say anything. I was disappointed. Then, she remembered, and asked if I would say a few words about my recent news. I mentioned instead the article on me in our college newspaper, as if the book wasn't a big deal to me. She said, "What Peter is too humble to mention is that he has a new book coming out." I smiled and turned red. I wonder if humility is more about appearances. I wonder about the fact that humility and humiliation share the same root. The fact that disgrace and shame are never far away from self-effacement and modesty. Both come from the Latin *humilis,* meaning low.

Nothing is more deceitful than the appearance of humility. It is often only carelessness of opinion, and sometimes an indirect boast.—Jane Austen

Sometimes I fear my entire life is made up of worrying about myself and pretending I'm not. I think that's why I like to fence. It's strange that athletics would be the place where I feel the most humble. Isn't sport all about ego? The desire to conquer? To be the best? To best your opponent? Maybe it is for most people, but fencing means something very different to me. Fencing is art. It's a dance. A chance to match the rhythm of my body with another. Though at one time I was ranked third in the U.S., I was never completely successful at developing the killer instinct needed in sport. I've lost many bouts even though I had superior technique and tactics, all because I didn't need to win bad enough, or perhaps that I sensed my opponent needed to win more. So, in place of the killer instinct, I devised a sort of philosophy where my goal was to fence my best in order to push my opponent to fence his best. I reasoned, if we both did that, I wouldn't care who wins. Wait. That's a lie. I still care. I still hurt. But I pretend I don't. Appearances again.

Early in life I had to choose between honest arrogance and hypocritical humility. I chose the former and have seen no reason to change.—Frank Lloyd Wright

I'd like to believe Frank Lloyd Wright spoke honestly. There is something refreshing about owning up to all the deceit. But I don't know. When someone openly admits to a lack of humility, doesn't it have the opposite effect? Isn't Frank Lloyd Wright just using a little reverse psychology on us, making us believe he is even more humble? If humility is pretense, then the most humble among us may be the most arrogant and the most arrogant among us the most humble because they are the most honest. Who would have thought Donald Trump to be the humblest man alive?

Humility is really important because it keeps you fresh and new.—Steven Tyler

Fencing erases the self. When I fence, time slows to a drip. When I fence, there is only my opponent before me. There is no thought. Only listening. Feeling the way his body moves. Watching it. Matching my rhythm to his. Waiting for the moment to strike. It's one of the only times I don't have the knot of anxiety in my stomach. The moment I enter the club door and smell that sour sweat from unwashed uniforms, hear the clang of steel, the screams of fencers as they release the energy from their attacks, I begin the process of shedding the skin of ego. I don my knickers, my jacket, my glove, and I'm almost there. By the time I grab my foil and put on my mask, I'm free. It's as if I'm reborn, at least for the two hours I'm in the club. When I was training for the U.S. team twenty years ago, I used to fence every night. A chance to erase myself every night. To make myself new. Now I fence once a week most of the time. Sometimes twice. The other five days living with my old self can be overwhelming.

I pray for humility, honestly, because it's very easy to be caught up in this world.—Katy Perry

Is that what ego is? Getting caught up in the world? And if so, is humility, then, by definition escaping this world, separating oneself from it? As Rumi says, *The soul sometimes leaves the body and then returns*

How does the world catch us? By reminding us that we are mortal? That we can fail? That we can hurt? That we can hurt others? Yes. To be human is to want. To be human is to fear. If we are honest, how much of our communication with others doesn't revolve around manipulation to get what we want or avoid what we fear? Everything from a baby's first cry to a child's pleading for a toy at Christmas to the adult telling his spouse "Whatever you want?" when clearly his body language suggests otherwise. The world demands we fight to survive and survival means asserting yourself over others. In this way, sport is honest. It makes no pretense about the battles we undertake every minute of every day. The athlete says directly and clearly, I will do everything I can to best you. Sometimes I think the ego is the only honest thing about us. Humility thrives in deceit. It feeds the illusion that we don't want and want and want.

Writing is another way of leaving the body, the body of the world. When I write, I don't want or fear anything, except for the next sentence to be good. For it to be true. And therein lies the rub. How few of those sentences are true. How few of them match the idea in my head. Writing offers up the greatest lesson in humility. The blank page the crucible where the ego melts away. There are only a handful of sentences I've written that I would stand behind and say, yes, therein lies truth. And that represents the published work and final drafts, many of which have been through dozens of revisions. Forget about all those early drafts and pieces that never made it. That means 99.9% of everything I've written is crap. Somewhere within it there is the stench of ego. The writer trying to sound pretty, to be profound, to be smarter than his reader, smarter than he really is. To hide his defects. If the above sentences are some of the true ones, then writing is not the ego free zone I'd thought.

Pride makes us artificial and humility makes us real.
—*Thomas Merton*

I think the percentage of true sentences I've written corresponds to the percentage of true moments in my life. Most of the time I'm trying to hide my fear that I'm not smart enough, not a good enough husband, a good enough father, my fear that I'm not handsome enough, not strong enough; in short, most of the time I feel like the nine year old boy who was left to care for his younger siblings, but didn't have the first clue on how to do it. And yet I pretend otherwise. What is this pretense? It's certainly not humility. When I pretend it's okay to do something I don't want to do, say for example to go out to eat or out dancing, is that humility? Or is it pride because I fear being seen as a bad husband? When I stand in front of an audience giving a paper at the Associated Writing Program's conference and make a self deprecating joke ending with something like "Of course, I don't really know what I'm talking about," is that humility? *You do not have to be good,* the poet Mary Oliver says. *You do not have to walk on your knees through the desert for a hundred miles, repenting.* And yet we do so desperately try to at least appear to be good.

There is no respect for others without humility in oneself.
—Henri Frederic Amiel

The other great lie is that we can actually love others, really love them. Love as a trick word. Marriage as deceit designed to ensure we don't die alone. We don't grow old alone. We don't raise our offspring alone. In short, we love so that we can believe we are not alone. And yet the history of art seems devoted to love, to portraying it as this unselfish thing, when in truth it is the most selfish thing of all. It's not that there aren't moments of respect, moments of true sacrifice, one lover for the other; it's just that those moments make up about the same number as my true sentences. At least, if we are honest. And we so rarely are. We so rarely respect another human being, not because we don't wish to, not because we don't try really, really hard, but because even while we're listening to that other (if we're listening at all) we're also fighting that thought that says what about me, what about my pain, my success, my story? What? You don't believe me? You must be one of the humble.

Mankind is like dogs, not gods—as long as you don't get mad they'll bite you—but stay mad and you'll never be bitten. Dogs don't respect humility and sorrow.
—Jack Kerouac

It's not to say we don't owe it to ourselves to try. To be the best we can be. But we also owe it to ourselves to be honest. To recognize how rarely we are not trying to manipulate a situation to put ourselves in the best light, how seldom we simply listen without offering our two cents. It's a necessity of survival. If we don't make sure people know who we are, what we're about, we'll be eaten alive.

Uncertainty is a sign of humility, and humility is just the ability or the willingness to learn.—Charlie Sheen

There are many in fencing who think it's all about bluster and bravado. There are athletes in all sports who think this. And to some extent they're right. But only partially so. For every victory won on bravado, there's another because the fencer opened to uncertainty. The athlete who leaves no room in his mind for doubt doesn't listen, doesn't stay open to the moment.

I didn't know to listen when I was a young fencer. I had to learn it when I came back to the sport at age forty-eight.

You just don't understand humility until you have children and get divorced.—Val Kilmer

My oldest daughter goes fencing with me every Monday. She loves to give me the evil eye when I limp back to the car after practice. She doesn't have to say anything. I know what she's thinking: *Dad, you're an idiot. Why do you still fence like your twenty? You know you can't keep doing this, Dad. You're going to hurt yourself.* Every time I get that look I think I understand the definition of humility. You never feel lower than when your own children out your foolish inconsistencies. Both my daughters also know I started my own Wikipedia page while drunk one night. They laugh about it hysterically at random times during dinner or when guests are over, and I shrivel and slink to a corner. My son gives me the look when I try to dance, or when I do anything to try to be cool. My son owns cool. At nine, it's okay to believe you own everything. I'm afraid to tell my children my worst mistakes. Afraid they would think less of me. I'm afraid some day they'll find out anyway. Is that pride? It's certainly not humility.

I claim to be a simple individual liable to err like any other fellow mortal. I own, however, that I have humility enough to confess my errors and to retrace my steps.—Mahatma Gandhi

If we confess our errors to ourselves is that humility? I don't know, but I fear it's not. Yet public apologies smack of pride and self-absorption. We all remember the weeping Jimmy Swaggart giving his "I have sinned" speech in 1988. Then there's Newt Gingrich's famous apology in which he partially defends his series of affairs on the grounds of his patriotism. And the list goes on: Arnold Schwarzenegger apologizing only after it was discovered he had a child with his maid, David Letterman apologizing only after he was blackmailed about his series of affairs with female interns, Tiger Woods apologizing only after he got caught, Bill Clinton apologizing only after lying repeatedly about his affair (even under oath), Rush Limbaugh apologizing regularly after offending someone (He offends someone nearly every day, but he doesn't always apologize for it). America has turned the public apology into grand theatre where insincerity reigns. "I'm sorry you were offended by my words…" So I wonder, is a bad apology really the opposite of humility? Is a bad apology worse than no apology at all?

Life is a long lesson in humility.—James M. Barried

Getting beat repeatedly by fencers much younger or older than you.

Telling your body to make a compound attack, and it refuses.

Telling your arm to make that parry and watching as it sits there like a petulant teen.

Telling your legs to retreat and falling on your ass instead.

Publishing a book but having no one review it.

Giving a reading of your new book and having no one show up.

Getting invited to a book club for your new book where no one has read it.

Reading what you think is the best thing you've written and looking up at the audience only to find their faces glazed over.

Reading what you think is the best thing you've written only to reread it the next day and realize it's crap.

Waking the next morning after fencing practice and not being able to walk.

Still not being able to walk a week later, or a month after that.

Having difficulty lifting your fencing bag and putting it in the car because your arthritis is acting up.

I thought all these things taught me humility.
I was wrong. They were simply signs of my lack of it.

Humility is knowing your health will never be the same again no matter what changes you make to your diet. Suddenly, you can't eat. Suddenly, you're laid up for days at a time all because your stomach says to hell with you.

Humility comes when you are hit in the face with something you can't control.

It's watching your daughter try and try to leave her room or to get dressed or to shower or get up for school or leave the house or do any number of things each of us takes for granted every moment of every day and be unable to because she suffers from an extreme form of OCD. To watch and not be able to do a damn thing about it.

It's seeing the resigned look in your son's face as he kneels down to play Legos alone yet again because you say you're too busy to play with him.

It's seeing the way your wife no longer bothers to ask you if you want to watch TV with her or talk with her or take a walk with her because she's tired of hearing your excuses.

Humility is realizing you are not the father you thought you were.

Not the husband you thought you were.

Not by a long shot.

We only really learn humility when faced with what we can't do. When overwhelmed by our own frailty, our own inability to be perfect. We understand it the day we realize we will never be as good as we once were, never as happy. And most especially when we realize how little we can do to help others understand the same thing.

Humility is the only true wisdom by which we prepare our minds for all the possible changes of life.—George Arliss

I imagine myself living a life of humility. It doesn't involve fencing. It doesn't involve the need to hurt myself, or push myself, to add another line to my CV. I think it would look something very much like this: I'm sitting in a recliner by the fire in our living room with the cats in my lap and the dogs at my feet. My wife sits reading on the couch next to me. My son plays with his Legos on the floor in front of me while my two daughters do their homework at the dining room table. I ask them about their day. I help them with questions about their homework. I play with my son on the floor and don't quit until he's tired of the game, then ask my wife if she'd like to take a walk. I could do that. I'm sure I could.

I would wake each morning and listen to my body. I would recognize the knot of anxiety in my stomach for what it is: the fear that I can't control my life, that often things happen and we can't do anything about them. I would take that knot out of my stomach, knead it into a ball, then flatten it and make cookies out of it. I would remember to forgive myself for not always being good. To forgive myself for not always being able to help my children.

I didn't realize that humility is tied to forgiveness, to forgiving others, but mostly to forgiving ourselves. There is something overly prideful about holding on to your pain, holding on to your sins.

Not being anxious requires a level of humility, doesn't it? It does, I think. It's not all about you.—Rupert Graves

Until now, I hadn't thought about pride as the need to be seen as good, the need to be seen as worthy. Of course, we are never worthy enough. Conversely, humility would be the knowledge that we can never be worthy. Our bodies know this. Our bodies are smarter than our brains. Our bodies know that search for worthiness is futile. They know our need for control is delusion. But because our brains try, our bodies get anxious. Like HAL in *2001: A Space Odyssey* our bodies can't compute the lie, and so they begin to break down. In surrendering to our bodies, saying yes to our bodies, we acknowledge that we are not worthy. We remind ourselves that we control very, very little. In surrendering, we allow for humility to enter our lives.

Expecting to be wrong about most things most of the time brings, finally, the kind of humility that leads to peace. I think.
—*John Burdett*

I tell my students I reserve the right to be wrong, that creative writing is an art, that there are no easy answers. But I wonder how often I show them I am wrong. Not often enough. And my kids? They come to me, and I try to have all the answers. *Daddy, can you fix this?* Of course. *Daddy, I'm afraid of the dark.* Let me cast a love spell over your room. *Daddy, I don't know how to let out my personality, to let people see who I truly am.* Let me tell you a story about someone who was also afraid to show who he was. I wonder, too, how often I tell my wife I'm wrong. We blame our spouses for our sins, when we should apologize. All the time. Let me say that again. We should apologize all the time. It goes hand in hand with accepting our unworthiness. *I could walk on my knees through the desert for a hundred miles, repenting*, and it would still not be apology enough. And to so many others. So many people I have wronged. It seems overwhelming to accept our role in the hurt of this world. As human beings, we resist. We don't want to be the ones to blame. It hurts, and we're already hurting so much. And yet. There it is. The pathway to humility clear as day.

Humility is attentive patience.—Simone Weil

And so we wait. Wait for humility to come to us. Wait to surrender. Wait for a time when it won't hurt quite so much to be wrong. For most of us that time never comes. There's always a reason. Even in sport there's always a reason. You can blame the ref, or you can blame your equipment. I once saw a fencer who couldn't take the pain of losing, the hurt from not being worthy, gather up all of his fencing equipment (bag, mask, jacket, knickers, glove, lamé, body cords, and foils) and throw it piece by piece in a trash can near the strip where he lost his last bout. He never came back for it. The best fencers, the best athletes don't make excuses. They accept their unworthiness in those moments when it arrives. They acknowledge that on this particular day, in this particular moment, their opponent bested them. The greatest athletes yearn for an opponent who can best them, one who will push them to be worthy.

Anything good in this life is worth waiting for. It takes a

long time. And humility may take the longest. Maybe we really don't ever know it until we feel the shock of pain in our chest, the pain that races up our left arm. The cold sweat that tells us our heart has stopped, and we are no more.

The job is to ask questions—it always was—and to ask them as inexorably as I can. And to face the absence of precise answers with a certain humility.—Arthur Miller

The thing I like most about writing is the fact that if I hit on a good story or essay I know I haven't answered a damn thing; rather, if I've done my job right, I've opened up a whole slew of questions in the reader. Of course, the absence of precise answers is the same thing as uncertainty in an athlete. A great athlete lives with the fact that he can be beaten at any time. He accepts that, and that is what pushes him to be even better. A writer, or any artist worth his salt, must live in that state, just as the best athletes must. The artist must live in the darkness of ambiguity. When a writer knows exactly what he or she is going to write, he or she is no longer a writer, but merely a typist. Creativity happens in the moment where the writer has no idea what comes next. The moment the writer enters the darkness of uncertainty. My life is well past the half way mark, and I'm embarrassed to say it took returning to fencing as an out of shape, old guy to make me understand that nothing is certain. Nothing is a given. Our bodies betray us in the end, as will our minds. All we can do is face the uncertainty with humility and hope we will find a way to pass through it. It has taken me this long to learn that I understand nothing. All we have left, if we are truly humble, is to question.

When it comes to true humility in the face of history, nothing beats complete silence.—Lev Grossman

Yes.

Bout Four:
Honesty

Every time somebody speaks of my honesty,
there is someone who quivers inside me.
                    Albert Camus

Yesterday, I took my nine-year-old son to the video arcade at the local mall. He wanted to play any game that involved shooting. I hadn't been to the video arcade since I was a teenager, so I was shocked to find so many realistic video games where the goal is to kill another human being. Fathers and sons fed their electronic game cards to the machines (they no longer accept quarters), shooting away, bonding as each looked to the other and smiled before wasting a "terrorist" or two or twenty in a bloody shootout. My son wanted to play, but I was appalled. I tried to get him interested in shooting dinosaurs instead. It worked for a short time, but in the end, he wanted to play the "real" games. I gave in and soon felt the kick of the machine gun recoil in my chest as I mowed down the terrorists (each bearded and colored just enough to look Muslim). My son was killed pretty quickly, but beamed at me, proud that I was able to survive a little longer.

Last Christmas, my son wanted a Nerf Diatron. It's a gun that shoots two Nerf discs at once; the latest technology in Nerf warfare. My son already has the other guns in the Nerf arsenal: the Vortex, the Nitron, the Vigilon, and (best of all) the Pyragon. Nerf gun wars erupt in our house spontaneously, causing our two German Shepherds to bark uncontrollably and the two kittens to run for cover. The only rule is no shooting in the face. Unfortunately, that's what inevitably happens. I get very uncomfortable when my son aims his gun at my face. I tell him in no uncertain terms to put it down. I tell him the game is over. And yet, when I sneak up on him defenseless, hiding behind the couch, I unleash my bullets at point blank range with a glee I haven't felt since childhood. In those moments, he looks at me as if I've betrayed him.

My son joined Karate about four months ago. He loves it. When not in practice, he spends a good part of his time running around the house, kicking and karate chopping everything. The day they broke boards in his dojo may have been the high point of his life. That's the day they tested for their belts. I had to hold back my judgment as I watched each student work through routines designed to beat the hell out of another living person. Some of the candidates for the higher belts were deadly serious as they performed their Katas. At the end, they had open sparring. The students wore headgear and gloves as they punched and kicked each other. My son is convinced he's going to be the next Bruce Lee. I told myself it wasn't so bad that he tried to kick another kid in the face. I forced myself to smile and clap when he performed actions designed to hurt or maim his opponent.

Because I've been an avid fencer most of my life, I tried to get my son involved in the sport of fencing about a year ago. He was interested in sabre at first, and I would drive him once a week to the club in Columbus where he could practice with kids his age. I remember the first time he suited up. I took a picture of him. I still have that picture. I look at it often, and each time it gives me a thrill. To see him posing with his mask and sword. He has since moved on to Karate, but I still hope to get him back into fencing. I dream of the day when he and I can travel to a fencing tournament together, when I can watch him fight another kid, trying to hit that kid in the head with his sword. Fencers scream when they hit, as do people in the other martial arts. I've often wondered what my son's scream would be like. Would it be relatively tame? Or would it let slip the killer inside?

Why is it I abhor the violence in one scenario and encourage it in another? What makes the simulated act of shooting "terrorists" in a video game any different than the simulated act of shooting each other with Nerf guns? Is hitting someone with your fist really more violent than hitting someone with a sword? One could easily argue it's the other way around. The sword a grim symbol of our barbaric past. And yet I frown upon one behavior and encourage another. Talk about sending mixed signals! I consider myself a passive person. I believe violence is a last resort, what happens when all other options fail. Contrary to the evidence given above, my wife and I raised our son without TV, video games, or violent toys. We gave in a couple years ago only when the mounting evidence became clear that none of what we did mattered. Regardless of our "guidance," he spent the vast majority of his day creating games where he killed someone or was killed by someone. The boy should be given an academy award for the complexity of his death scenes, drawn out in slow motion as he careens about the living room. My fear is that some day he'll enlist in the military, that he'll become something I'm fundamentally against. My greater fear is that in doing so he'll become more like me than he ever was before.

I remember playing with little green plastic army men when I was a kid. I'd use Legos to make elaborate buildings and cityscapes the army men could move through, places they could hide behind as they shot each other. I was particularly violent with insects, using Black Cats to blow up ant holes or stink bugs, launching grasshoppers into space in my Estes Rockets or doing biomedical experiments on them. My two personal favorites involved measuring how long a grasshopper could last being heated in the microwave or seeing how long it could be frozen and still live once I thawed it out.

Despite my tendency to play Dr. Mengele with insects, I was not a bully. In fact, most of my childhood memories involve being bullied by others. But I did fight back when it got to be too much. Danny Zangari and Kevin Blixt were particularly relentless. One day, behind the elementary school library, after they'd been pushing and teasing me, I told them I'd had it, saying those fateful words: "I Choose You," which basically meant, "Let's Fight." The rumble was arranged for after school. I'd had second thoughts and tried to sneak out the back door. Danny Zangari's gang was waiting. They surrounded me and walked me out to the field away from adult interference. When I got there, I whipped around and shoved Danny Zangari to the ground, then took off running. The gang gave chase, including one Craig Schroeder who vied with me for the title of fastest runner in the fourth grade. I could easily outrun them all, except for Craig Schroeder. I don't know why he chased me so hard. I remember feeling a bit betrayed by it. I hadn't realized he was friends with my rivals. I wonder now if his betrayal had anything to do with friendship. Rather, I think it was simply another chance to prove he was the fastest runner, except he wasn't. He couldn't catch me, and when in desperation he made a diving grab for me in front of the playground equipment, I dodged to the right and he slammed into the jungle gym. I can still hear his surprised scream.

I twice punched other bullies in elementary school, though not in self-defense. I'd come to the aid of my sister and my friend respectively. Strangely, the only time I fought back physically was when others were threatened.

I continued my pattern of running away from bullies all through middle school and high school. Though I dreamed of fighting back. I often imagined turning on the unsuspecting bully, grabbing him by the throat and ramming him up against the gym lockers, then slowly raising him above my head like some superhuman. In my dream scenario, I would tell him to leave me the hell alone or the next time I wouldn't be responsible for what happened. My nine-year-old son has had trouble with bullies for the past two years. He told me this morning that he was bringing a book to school with a girl on the cover. He said that if the bullies teased him about it, he would open the book and show them a scene where they kill something

When I started fencing at the age of eighteen, my parents didn't understand because they thought I'd never been a violent child. As my fencing obsession continued, my mother worried that it would increase my testosterone levels and therefore make me more violent. To some extent, I think she was right. For a very long time, I didn't think I had the killer instinct. I didn't think I could get angry. I didn't think I had the desire to dominate my opponent. Those were lies. All of it was there, often unleashed in my dreams. The most common dreams I had growing up were extraordinarily violent as I would inevitably find myself fighting several people with my sword, stabbing them over and over. I still remember the squishing sound as my sword plunged into their bodies, the suck as I pulled it out, and the satisfaction I felt as I watched the life ebb from their faces.

I'm pretty sure all those years of fencing put me in touch with the part of myself that was able to express anger, a part I'd repressed since childhood. No one in my family was allowed to show anger, at least no one except my father. We were required to be happy all the time. Going back to fencing at forty-eight, I was amazed at how easily I could tap into the cold-blooded heart of the killer. When I hit my opponent, my yell was more animal than human. The army has it right. You can train someone to be a killer. Anyone.

In my case, my training helped me to survive my second marriage. My wife has a temper. My earliest memories of our relationship are of the fact that I needed to get tough if I was going to make it. I needed to fight back. And fight back I did. My wife and I have cultivated the ability to go for the jugular. We are probably the only couple in history who weren't horrified by the film version of Edward Albee's *Whose Afraid of Virginia Woolf?* In fact, we said something like, "Wow, that seems a lot like us!"

My kids now call me "The Volcano." It's as if years of repression combined with a marriage that cultivated quick fight or flight reflexes have led to uncontrollable explosions of anger. I have reached the point where I no longer understand the things we do to each other, to those we love. My wife and I can go from zero to sixty in an argument in two point three seconds. We have crossed the line so many times it no longer exists. When we talk of honesty, we need to talk about the promises we make to those we supposedly love. The promise to nourish, honor and respect, rather than poison, cut, and destroy. The promise to our children that we will provide a safe home in which they don't have to worry about one parent or the other exploding. We have to talk about the lie that says we aren't violent when evidence of that violence saturates every aspect of our lives from the Bush Doctrine and Abu Ghraib to sporting events in which fighting has become an expected part of the "entertainment," from nightly news casts that seem nothing more than body counts—tonight it's the cops shooting the un armed man, tomorrow it's the kid shooting the cops—to an entertainment industry that seems to think the only way to create conflict in a story is to have someone shoot, stab, or crush someone else. According to the Senate Committee on the Judiciary's 1999 report on "Children, Violence, and the Media," by the time the average child is eighteen years old he or she will have witnessed 18,000 murders and 200,000 acts of violence. Of course, the consistent denial of our violence is not our only deceit. Another lie festers deep in our American psyche. We haven't charted how many images of "happily ever after" our children see on TV or movies or read about in books and magazines, but I'd wager it's equally high. Of course, there's nothing wrong with trying to put a positive face on marriage, but we can do better in our education than the simplistic story that finding Mr. or Mrs. Right will solve all your problems. Honesty is acknowledging that for every day your spouse makes your morning coffee or takes your hand as you sit together watching TV, there is another where he or she plans your murder.

What might an honest picture of human relationships look like? My guess is it would look a lot like a fencing bout. In fencing, your goal is to disguise your intent. When you're attacking, you want to make it look as if you're not attacking. When you're setting a trap, you want to appear as if you've let your guard down. Everything is, in essence, a manipulation of your opponent. If you do make a simple straight attack—in other words an "honest" move—it's to set up your second intention of a counter-riposte to the heart, made after you've carefully created an expectation in your opponent that you were only capable of feints. When my wife goes to the other room and closes the door in order to "read a book," I ask her what she's doing, when I really want to ask why she's mad at me. When my wife wants to read this essay, she tells me it's because she's genuinely interested, but what she really wants is to see how she's represented in it. How rarely do we say what we mean. When we do, it's a sudden thrust to the chest, designed to catch our opponent off guard, designed for maximum damage. "I hate your guts," or "You're a fucking freak." The coupe de grace comes when feints and ruses are no longer necessary, or, perhaps, when they've lost their power. It's the same in any relationship, even the most sacred relationship of all, that of parent/child. The one relationship where we should be honest. I'm not talking about the countless times we tell our children everything will be all right when we know damn well it won't be, or the times when we say "Great job!" when of course it was only mediocre. I'm talking about the times we tell our children to take their medicine not because they need it but because we need it, because we need a moment of peace. Or the times we tell them to practice their music or work harder in school not because we know it will be good for them (which is part of it) but because we want them to look good for us, to represent us well (which is also part of it). At least in a fencing bout we are honest about the manipulation. Both parties arrive on the strip knowing that each will do his or her best to trick the other. Sometimes I think we lie so often to our spouses and loved ones because we are already lying to ourselves about what we want. How can you be truthful with others if you are not truthful with yourself? We say we want a wife and kids, maybe a dog or two. A house in a good neighborhood with good schools. A job that allows us to provide for our family. When really what we want is to live in a bare apartment on our own and write. Or to start a theatre company and collaborate with other artists. Or maybe we don't want that. Maybe that's a trick of the mind, too. Or maybe we want all these things and the problem is that their importance changes from day to day. We lie simply because we can't keep track of our shifting desire.

I have always thought of myself as a passive person. I've also always thought of myself as honest. And yet I lie everyday. Mainly to myself. Or is that another lie? I'm an empathetic person. At least I like to think so. My therapist says my empathic meter is off the charts but that the meter of my own feelings is broken. I'm really good at sensing what other people need and then being that thing. The only problem is that if you do that long enough you forget who you are. You become an onion, each lie another layer, and it becomes more and more difficult to find anything at the center. Which may be why I returned to fencing at a time when my body was starting to rot. I don't have to be anyone else when I fence, and therefore, I know who I am. My only job is to sense my opponent's weaknesses, to feel them out and exploit them. I used to be uncomfortable with this, with the violence of it. The thoughts that ran through my head. The need to stab my opponent. The inevitable anger that erupted at a bad call or when my opponent played dirty or yelled a bit too loudly in my face. But then I learned that I could harness that anger into a deadly double coupé attack. And more recently I've realized that as much as I hate to admit it, violence may be the one form of human communication where we are completely and utterly honest. As a pacifist, I don't like this. Not one bit. But that doesn't make it any less true. Civility is a construct designed to keep us from offing one another. It is essential that we lie about our nature in order to be better human beings. But being better human beings doesn't mean we are more truthful.

The idealist in me wants to say that love is the one pure emotion. The cynic in me says that's a lie. Love is adulterated by our desire to be loved. And we will do just about anything to be loved, including, as has often been the case in human history, committing acts of violence. The samurai understood the relationship between honesty and violence. They knew that we can't run from who we are. It doesn't mean we indulge our violent natures or even embrace them, but we do have to accept them. Cormac McCarthy says that he writes such violent books because he believes we too often try to hide from our violent natures, and by doing so we are doomed to be slaves to them. It's difficult to look at ourselves honestly. Maybe that's one reason civilization has grown around us as it has, so that we won't have to look too closely at ourselves. We can pretend to be this other thing. So we create institutions like marriage and pretend human beings were meant to live together their entire lives. We create a legal system so that we don't resort to *Holmgang* as the Vikings did, a system where disputes were solved by a duel. Might makes right!

When I first returned to fencing at nearly a half-century of age, I thought I might be running from myself. I'd wanted out of my marriage. I wanted to restructure my life around the life of the artist. I couldn't stand to sit alone with myself because I felt my life was a lie.

I was wrong.

I thought my marriage had to be perfect. I thought my wife had to be as driven and deluded as me.

I was wrong.

On the strip it became clear. When I stood *en-garde* I looked closely at my masked opponent and saw myself. I saw a man who was not good, though he'd told himself he had to be good, always. I saw a man capable of hurting others. I saw a man capable of violence toward others. A man willing to lie. A man willing to cheat. I saw a man who was tired and afraid of growing old, afraid of what it might mean if he'd made the wrong decisions, if he'd wasted his life.

The samurai believed that the first man to attack in combat was inevitably the loser. Samurai combats were famous for the fact that the entire battle took place as the two stared each other down, each knowing it would be the one who was afraid who would attack first. I have been afraid. I have known what it is like to fear mortality, to fear being alone, to fear being inauthentic. The samurai accepted the possibility of their own death. They accepted the violence within them. They accepted the fact that the longer they faced off against their opponent, the more honest they became. Marriage, if it lasts, teaches us that. The longer we face off against our spouse, the more we realize the trouble is not with them, but with us. Until we accept that, we are doomed to live a lie. Accepting the threat of violence teaches that, too. Not the threat from the other but from within ourselves.

Bout Five:
Mercy

Dreaming of Mercy St.
Wear your inside out
Dreaming of mercy
In your daddy's arms again . . .

"Mercy Street" by Peter Gabriel

When I first began fencing, I often let my opponent win. This seems like a shocking confession coming from someone who has spent the majority of his life trying to make it to the top of his sport. If I sensed that my opponent might be too upset by losing, I would let up on them. In other words, I would show mercy.

At the Battle of Jaffa, When King Richard the Lionheart's horse was killed and he was forced to battle on foot, Saladin, the first sultan of Egypt and Syria, sent him two of his own horses, so he could continue fighting with honor. The Crusaders then went on to win the battle.

"Mercy" defined as showing compassion or forgiveness toward someone to whom it is in one's power to punish or do harm. Would it have done "harm" to my opponent if I beat him? I thought so at the time based on the way in which he would storm up and down the strip, as if the very possibility of losing might cause him to explode.

A crucial component of the definition of mercy is that you cannot show it unless you already hold power over another. The impoverished and disenfranchised cannot show mercy by definition.

I had to get over the tendency to let my opponents win pretty quickly if I was going to be a successful athlete, and I wanted to be a successful athlete. I dreamed of going to the Olympics. A successful athlete has to crush his opponents, to dominate them. It is expected. It is, in fact, rewarded. And so it was not enough to beat my opponents, I needed to beat them as badly as possible. To skunk them. To "bagel" them. The bagel being the shape of a zero. My goal was to make sure my opponents didn't score a touch. You can't afford mercy if you want to breed fear.

It's not surprising I was able to get past my desire to show mercy so quickly. It's difficult to be human on planet earth without failing to show mercy somewhere along the line. There was the time when I was eleven and I shot the injured bird over and over again with a pea-shooter. It couldn't fly away, and so I kept blowing kernels of corn through my straw. Each time, it looked at me and chirped, and I was sure it was asking why. Not that I could answer. Children learn quickly when they must show mercy and when they can get away with leaving it in the dust.

I've often wondered how many times the fact that I beat someone in fencing for an important bout may have changed their lives. Did they ever give up on their dream as a result? I do know one fencer who still reminds me twenty years later that he only came to the realization it was time to quit after I destroyed him 5-0, 5-0 for the second tournament in a row. Was my lack of mercy a favor or a curse? I know that when I lost the bout that lost me the world championship team in 1994, I returned to my hotel room and threw up. I sometimes wonder if I've ever recovered from that loss. But would I have wanted my opponent to show mercy? I don't think so.

Mercy from the Latin "price paid or wages" as in *merc, merxi*—*"merchandise."* When we show mercy to another are we earning something or is it the price paid for living?

There are moments when we might wish to show mercy but we cannot. Another bird from my youth. This time the bird was caught in a freshly tarred road. I should have killed it. Put it out of its misery. But I couldn't bring myself to do it. I thought about riding my bike over it, hitting it with a stick, a rock. I rode my bike toward it but slammed on the brakes at the last second. I held the rock over its head but couldn't bring it down. What stayed my hand was imagining its suffering if I didn't happen to kill it right away. So, I let it suffer more.

When we fail to show mercy what price is paid?

I overcame my tendency to let my opponent win by cultivating a philosophy wherein I was really showing mercy by fencing my best. In my admittedly warped view, I rationalized that if I fenced to the best of my ability, I would give my opponent the chance to fence to the best of his ability. In my line of reasoning, I would actually do more harm to my opponent by fencing poorly. I am not a republican. Politically, I'm as far to the left as you can go, but I sometimes wonder if my fencing philosophy has a little too much in common with the Horatio Alger story of picking yourself up by your bootstraps. The best thing for you is to get beaten. You can't grow into a whole human being if you're given a handout. I'm not very comfortable with this.

Welfare spending is about half what the U.S. government forks out in subsidies to big corporations.[1] Three hundred of the most profitable companies in the U.S. pay a tax rate of half the corporate rate of 35%. Thirty of the most profitable companies have a negative income tax rate even though they took home a combined profit of 160 billion dollars.[2] It's clear we don't expect corporations to pull themselves up by their bootstraps.

In the Parable of the Prodigal Son (Luke 15: 11-32), Jesus describes fatherly mercy as a "gratuitous, generous gift."

When I went back to school for an MFA in creative writing at age 37 after finally realizing what I wanted to do with my life, my parents let me know that if I hit some rough spots financially, they would be there to help. Their "handouts" allowed me to get through school and turn my life around. I never felt like less of a person because I accepted their money. Nor did taking their money diminish my understanding of the importance of earning my own way. If anything, it made me more determined to prove myself and show that their investment in me was not in vain.

In Ephesians: 2-4, the Apostle Paul refers to the mercy of God in terms of salvation: "God, being rich in mercy . . . even when we were dead through our sins, made us alive together with Christ." Here mercy has the power to transform, to resurrect the metaphoric dead. The one who has mercy, in this case God, must be rich, if he is to bestow these riches, this "price paid" on others.

According to the *New York Times*, the actual figure for the corporate bailouts of the first decade of the 21st century is closer to twelve trillion dollars.[3] Strangely, we don't expect corporations to learn what it means to earn their own way. We say about big corporations, "When they fail, we all fail." Why don't we apply this same logic to individuals? But wait, the Supreme Court ruled that corporations *are* individuals, so in a strange way we do.

St. Peter writes in Peter 2:9-10, "But ye are a chosen generation, a royal priesthood, an holy nation, a peculiar people; that ye should shew forth the praises of him who hath called you out of darkness into his marvelous light; Which in times past were not a people, but are now the people of God: which had not obtained mercy, but now have obtained mercy." God showed his infinite mercy through the ultimate "price paid," that of his son.

Kyrie eleison, Christe eleison . . . Lord have mercy, Christ have mercy.

When we look to make cuts, we feel lucky that the government cuts only 8 billion from food stamps instead of the proposed 39 billion.[4] The same government that passed a 600 billion plus war budget the same year. We'd rather drop bombs in the night on a distant people through a proxy war than feed our own poor.

In the Torah, mercy is one of the attributes of God. In one of the central revelations at Sinai in 2 Exodus 34:6, "the Lord is a merciful and gracious God, slow to anger, abounding in steadfast love and faithfulness."

It's easier to fail at showing mercy when the one to whom we should show it is a nameless, faceless group.

In Islam, the title "the Most Merciful" (al-Rahman) is one of the names of Allah.

Yin, the goddess of mercy, is one of the most venerated Bodhisattva.

We can label them, shape them into the image of the "welfare queen" or "terrorists," or simply "those people," and then we can quietly and calmly turn our backs, or bomb them.

In Plutarch's lives, he tells of how when Alcyoneus killed Pyrrhus, he took the head back to his father, Antigonus. When Antigonus saw the head, he hit his son with his staff and drove him away, calling him barbarous. He took careful pains to properly bury his enemy's head.

In *The Metamorphoses,* Ovid speaks of how Perseus cared for the head of Medusa after he chopped it off. "He makes the ground soft with a bed of leaves, and on top of that he strews little branches of plants born under water, and on this he places Medusa's head, face down."

My brother gave me his head to care for when he went through difficult times with his teenage daughter and later with his marriage. He opened his pain to me. I did not lay that head down in the grass, but instead offered advice.

I lost my way. I forgot to call your name.[5]

The greatest power we have over one another is whether or not we listen.

I don't listen often enough in my marriage.

Or with my kids.

My oldest daughter says the only time I hear her is when I ask if she's done her homework and practiced her harp.

My son says I never hear him.

My wife says I don't know who she is and what she wants.

I say the same thing to her.

How, then, can we be merciful?

the words
they fade
I sift
toward other languages
you must listen
with your hands
with the twist ends
of your hair . . .[6]

The relationship between coach and fencer is the most intimate in sport. It's the most intimate relationship I know. Fencers are proud of the fact that the only thing that moves faster than the tip of the sword is a bullet leaving a gun. The sport relies on quick reflexes trained in the body and the body's ability to listen to that of another. To train the fencer, the coach must understand him better than he understands himself. He must know how his student's body will react in stress. How he will react when he has a big lead. How he will react when the opponent yells in his face, or if the ref reverses a call.

The first time I made a North American Cup final, I fenced better than I'd ever done before. I nearly beat the reigning national champion. Many people thought I did beat him. They thought the ref screwed me on the calls. I actually scored more points than my opponent, but it was possible back then to score more points and still lose the match: 5-1, 5-6, 5-6. The point is that before the tournament my coach told me that he'd overheard another coach say I didn't have it in me to win. That I was technically good, but didn't have the killer instinct. It pissed me off. My coach knew it would piss me off. That's why he told me.

I'm still very close with both my fencing coaches. We've shared the same bed while traveling to tournaments. We've cried on each other's shoulders as each of us has gone through divorce, mid-life crises, fears for our children. It's strange because ninety-nine percent of our interactions have been on the fencing strip, dealing only with the body. My listening for his cue to attack. His reading the contour of my shoulder to see if it's tense. My listening for the patterns in his footwork to know when to attack. His reading the angle of my foil to judge when I'm tired.

I say it again. It is a precondition of mercy that you have to listen.

After Hurricane Katrina, the poverty displayed on TV was a surprise to many people in the U.S. despite the fact that fifty million Americans live below the poverty line.[7] That's about 16% of the population.

I stopped to listen but he did not come.[8]

Most of us have trouble seeing ourselves clearly, much less our neighbor. I have to laugh how often athletes blame the refs or the equipment or some other external factor for their loss. Fencing is subjective. The ref has to decide who started the attack first in a sport where the difference between who started may be $1/100^{th}$ of a second. So, it's easy for a fencer to blame the ref.

I've seen fencers throw their masks or their foils across the room over bad calls. One fencer spewed forth a string of F bombs the like of which I hadn't heard before or since. Another fencer, a proud recon Marine, collapsed on the ground sobbing after arguing a call for an hour. The coaches and parents are often worse. They throw chairs, knock over barricades, get in the ref's face and threaten him or her verbally. Rarely, if ever, do these fencers and coaches look at themselves and say maybe my attack wasn't executed perfectly enough, or maybe I didn't teach my fencer well enough to execute his attack so that the ref could clearly see it. The fault always lies with the other. This is a lack of mercy, but not toward the ref. It is a lack of mercy toward ourselves.

Of course, that's why I'm here. That's why we're all here. Life teaches us nothing if not, in the end, to take a good, long look at ourselves. Maybe we are afraid to because we know mercy may not be forthcoming. If it's difficult to show mercy to another, it's darn near impossible to show it toward oneself.

I've often wondered if the relentless pace at which I drive myself is because I hate who I am, or at the very least am distinctly uncomfortable with that person. Better to keep moving than to stop and look in the mirror. The trouble is I'm finding it difficult to keep the pace as I get older, though it's more important than ever to avoid that mirror.

It's never easy to practice mercy, but it's easier when we're young. Before we've piled up a lifetime of mistakes. Before we lie. Before we fall short of our dream. Before we have affairs. Before we divorce. Before we do not speak our mind when we see problems in our brother's marriage. Before we do speak our mind when we see problems in our brother's marriage. Before we fail to be the person we thought we would be. Before we live a lie. Before we forget who we are. Before we remember who we are. Before our children discover who we are. Before we fail to become the person our spouse wants us to be. Before each day of our lives simply becomes another strand in the rope.

Who can listen to the music of a life and not feel a little bit deceived?

When I returned to fencing at forty-eight, I pushed myself as if I was still young. Nothing too abnormal there. Lots of middle-aged, arm-chair athletes overdo it when they try to regain their youth in sport. But I didn't stop. Not when my pulled hip extensor made it difficult to walk. Not when the sciatica in my back made it difficult to sit. Not when the arthritis in my hand made it difficult to hold a glass or pick up my laptop. Not when the torn rotator cuff in my shoulder made it nearly impossible to get dressed. I didn't slow down a beat. In fact, I wanted to hurt. No mercy.

And so I fence. I plug my foil into the electric reel, march onto the strip, salute my opponent, then try to stab him. I study the other fencers on the veteran circuit. Many of them older than me. And I wonder why they do it. I've watched the grace of a seventy plus year old woman fencing against people half and a third and a fourth her age. I've studied how after each loss she smiled and shook her opponent's hand then quietly walked back to her chair to sit and wait patiently for her next bout. She wasn't in my pool. I didn't have to fence her, but I can't help wonder what might have happened if I did. Would I have let her win? Would I have risked messing up my indicators, my seating, all so that she could have a victory? I'd like to think I would have, but I'm not sure. Would it have mattered to her if she'd won? I don't think so. I'd like to think she's beyond that. Beyond the need to hurt herself. To hurt others.

You see I have trouble not being good. A good person. Good at what I do. I'm uncomfortable when life gets messy. No scratch that. I'm uncomfortable when I get messy, my feelings get messy, and I no longer understand what being good means. Getting older is not about getting wiser. Getting older is about realizing you don't understand anything, coming to terms with that fact, and then forgiving yourself for your stupidity.

Forgiveness as a precondition for mercy.

I come home at night with the best of intentions. I'm going to take a walk with my wife. We'll talk about things besides the kids. We'll listen to each other's story. But then we face off and the effect of all those years of crossing the line shows itself in the way we no longer look directly at each other, or the way we don't quite smile when the other walks into the room, the way in which the conversation is always stilted because we're each so busy looking for the poison laced within the words of the other.

Even if we could begin to unravel the complex game in which we find ourselves, the moment is lost as first one child and then another demands our attention. The daughter with OCD needs help getting into her room, or out of her room, or getting her glasses, or taking off her glasses. The other daughter needs to be reeled in, to be called back from the swing, or the basement, or the book, or the TV screen, whatever it is she's chosen to shield herself with from the daily tension. The ten-year-old son needs help with his homework, or needs you to explain why he should go to school at all when he hates it so much.

I try to explain the homework. I try to explain why my daughter needs to be part of the family. I try to reconcile the fact that OCD has stolen so much of my other daughter's life. I try to talk to my wife, to explain why my best intentions always seem to fail. And I keep coming up short. She says I'm more of a father than a husband. She says I understand nothing.

And she's right.
I don't even understand who I am.
I can't forgive myself for that.
To live in the mercy of God. The complete
sentence too adequate, has no give.[9]

If we don't even understand ourselves, maybe we shouldn't judge other people that harshly. Maybe we should grant them the possibility that they, too, are living, and therefore, suffering, doing everything they can to forgive themselves and most probably failing.

The only mercy is memory.[10]
Let us pray for the forgetfulness of sleep.

Notes

1. Huffington Post: Business. "Welfare Spending Nearly Half What U.S. Forked Out in Corporate Subsidies in 2006." http://www.huffingtonpost.com/2012/09/25/government-subsidies-corporations_n_1912835.html (accessed October 1, 2014).

2. Huffington Post: Business. "Thirty of U.S.'s Most Profitable Companies Paid "Less Than Zero" in Income Taxes in Last 3 Years." http://www.huffingtonpost.com/2011/11/03/major-corporations-tax-subsidies_n_1073548.html (accessed October 1, 2014).

3. The New York Times. "Adding Up the Government's Total Bailout Tab." http://www.nytimes.com/interactive/2009/02/04/business/20090205-bailout-totals-graphic.html?_r=0 (accessed October 1, 2014).

4. Wright, D.S. FDL Newsdesk. "House Farm Bill Includes 8 Billion of Cuts to Food Stamps." http://news.firedoglake.com/2014/02/03/house-farm-bill-includes-8-billion-of-cuts-to-food-stamps/ (accessed October 1, 2014).

5. Cohen, Leonard, *The Book of Mercy*

6. Clifton, Lucille, "out of body," from *Mercy* (Rochester: BOA Editions, 2004).

7. Clyne, Melissa. Newsmax. "Americans Living Below Poverty Line Hits Record Under Obama." http://www.newsmax.com/Newsfront/poverty-line-grows-under/2014/01/08/id/545892 (accessed October 1, 2014).

8. Cohen, Leonard, *The Book of Mercy*

9. Levertov, Denise, "To Live in the Mercy of God," from *Sands from the Well* (New York: New Directions, 1986).

10. Clifton, Lucille, epigraph from *Mercy* (Rochester: BOA Editions, 2004).

Bout Six:
Loyalty

All men are loyal, but their objects of allegiance are at best approximate.

John Barth

CHARACTERS

Peter Grandbois—a forty-nine year old professor of creative writing at a small liberal arts college. He is married and has three children, two dogs, two cats, and an aquarium full of fish. For him, the year is 2014, the year he is granted tenure.

Alexander (Sasha) Romankov—Five time world champion foil fencer from the former Soviet Union, considered by many to be the greatest fencer in history. As a member of the Soviet military, he prides himself on precision and discipline in everything. For him it is 1983, the year before the Olympics in which he is favored to win, the year before the Soviet Union will boycott those same Olympics. He is thirty years old and has just won his fifth world championship title.

Kobo Abe—Japanese novelist and playwright, most famous for his novel *Woman in the Dunes*. The quintessential artist, he is married to a painter, and has established his own theatre company. He is known for his surreal, almost nightmarish explorations of individuals trapped in contemporary society. For him, it is 1993, the year of his death. He is sixty-nine years old. He has been several times nominated for a Nobel Prize but never won.

$\mathcal{S}$etting: A café at a small town in the Midwest. It is early morning.

(The scene opens with KOBO and SASHA siting on opposite sides of a table in the corner of the café. They've finished their espressos and are now turned away from each other and staring in opposite directions. Sasha checks his watch while Kobo doodles on a napkin. PETER arrives flustered with his mug of tea.)

Sasha: You're half an hour late

Peter: (sitting) Sorry. One of the dogs had diarrhea. You wouldn't believe the mess. Then, my son forgot his lunch. I had to drop it by the school.

Kobo: He'll never learn that way.

Sasha: (nodding his head) He's right.

Peter: The dog or the boy?

(Kobo and Sasha simply shake their heads.)

Kobo: My father was strict in all things.

Sasha: Your father wanted you to become a doctor and look what happened.

Peter: Listen. Before we start, I need to know. Did either of you have children?

Kobo: You brought us here to ask us that?

Peter: I've been searching the Internet all morning in preparation for this meeting, and I can't find out anything.

Sasha: I thought this breakfast meeting was to discuss your subpar footwork. Aren't you trying to get back into fencing?

Peter: Well, yeah . . . I'd love any pointers you have for . . .

Kobo: I thought you wanted to talk about playwriting. A life in theatre.

Peter: That, too. I feel so lonely as a novelist. What's it like to collaborate with . . .

Sasha: You don't know what you want, do you? I should have known. Stupid American!

Kobo: Wait a second. He has a lot of interests. Maybe it's a sign of brilliance.

Sasha: Brilliance is a perfectly executed direct attack. It's something demonstrated. Proven. You know it when you see it.

Kobo: The simple mindedness of the military man!

Sasha: Nothing worth knowing can be understood with the mind. Truth lies in the body.

Kobo: On that we might agree. Though the body can also lead us astray.

Sasha: Nonsense!

Peter: Look! It wasn't easy getting you two here. I had to pull a lot of strings in the space/time continuum. So, can we please not argue!

Sasha: You've got to pick your loyalties. You say you want the life of an artist. You also want to be a great fencer, and you want a family.

Kobo: Jack of all trades, master of none.

Sasha: Exactly.

Peter: I don't understand.

Sasha: Of course you don't. You think like an American. You think you can have it all. You think all you have to do is try and the world will lie down at your feet.

Peter: How did *you* do it? How did you stay so dedicated to your craft?

Kobo: Sacrifice.

Sasha: Da. You have to kill what you love.

Kobo: Dedication is a harsh mistress.

Sasha: Anything gets in your way, stab the fucker!

Kobo: I don't know if I'd go that far.

Sasha: Because you're soft.

Kobo: You try living in Japan after the war, much less trying to write!

Sasha: You're almost as bad as him. (He nods to Peter) With your medical degree. All that wasted time!

Kobo: I won't even dignify that with an answer. (Kobo takes another napkin and begins drawing something furiously.)

Peter: You didn't answer my earlier question. Do either of you have children? Do you have a family?

(Kobo continues drawing. Sasha crosses his arms and stares at Peter, shaking his head.)

Peter: See, if you're talking about killing your hobbies, or your girlfriends—I'm being metaphorical of course—or the job you hate, your TV habit, the friendships that suck up your time, I think I understand, but if it's your family . . . well, that's what I want to know. What if it's your family?

Sasha: Life is messy.

(Kobo holds up his napkin. We see a drawing of two men fencing, one with a pen, the other with a sword. The man with the pen has just stabbed the man with the sword. Blood spurts from the wound.)

Sasha: Very funny.

Kobo: The artist is loyal to his art. There is nothing else.

Peter: Bullshit! What about life? What about the fact that the artist has to live life, to experience it if he's ever going to write about it?

Kobo: You've been reading too much Hemingway. He "lived" life and look where it got him. Three marriages. A drunk. Dead.

Sasha: Don't forget the Nobel Prize.

Kobo: What's that supposed to mean?

Sasha: Nothing. It's just that you've been nominated so often . . . and you're not getting any younger.

Kobo: How dare you!

Peter: Can we please stay focused? I don't want to talk about Hemingway, or Nobel Prizes, or . . .

Sasha: Are you going to be loyal to yourself or to others?

Kobo: That's really the only question.

Peter: Can't I be both?

Sasha: You really are stupid, aren't you?

Kobo: Don't be so hard on him, Sasha. Let the kid try.

Sasha: There's one good thing about the Soviet system. It eliminates choice. I knew from the moment I could walk, that I would be a fencer. My first memories are of holding a sword in my hand.

Kobo: Doesn't lack of choice also eliminate passion?

Peter: Yes . . . If you're going to have real passion, it's got to be because it's something you choose to do.

Sasha: More American brainwashing. (Shaking his head at Kobo) I'm surprised at you. You should know better than anyone that devotion creates passion. Time and discipline are passion's muses. Haven't you heard of the ten thousand hour rule?

Kobo: I don't think I could have ever become passionate about medical school.

Sasha: (laughing) You flunked out three times!

Kobo: That choice was made for me by my father.
Sasha: Had you stayed, had you put in the time, devoted

yourself to it, you would have found the passion.

Kobo: (almost to himself) I'm not so sure.

Peter: There's a big difference between choosing to do something and being forced to do something.

Sasha: But let's be honest, Peter, no one forced you to have a family. No parent told you to raise children or you'd be disinherited.

Peter: I know. I know. I don't mean that.

Kobo: Are you sure?

Sasha: Because it sounds like you're making excuses.

Peter: What I mean is that there's a gray area between choosing and being forced…and sometimes that gray area gets . . .

Kobo: Messy?

Peter: Yes!

Sasha: Gray areas are just another American contrivance. A

convenient excuse. They allow you to overthink. The truth is you want it all, Peter. You're not willing to sacrifice. To kill what gets in the way. No wonder you were only a mediocre fencer.

Peter: Wait a second! That's not fair. And besides, I was pretty good.

Sasha: Mediocre.

Peter: You don't know! You can't know because you never had children.

Sasha: How do you know I don't have children?

Kobo: Yes, how do you know?

Peter: I mean . . . do you or don't you?

Kobo: Why is it so important? You have to live for yourself.

Sasha: Find out for yourself. You can't live another person's life.

Kobo: You can't look for models.

Sasha: I could be the best father, the best husband alive, but that's not what it's about. That's not your story.

Kobo: Or maybe I ignored my children. They all grew up unhappy, and now they hate me. That's not the point.

Peter: Then what is?

Sasha: The point is that you so desperately need it to matter. The point is that you're trying to live like everyone else instead of listening to yourself.

Peter: I don't get it. I thought we were going to meet here to talk about what it means to be loyal to your craft, to others.

Kobo: You have to be loyal to yourself.

Peter: But what if I don't like myself?
What if this self is not who I want to be?

Sasha: Grow up! Nobody likes themselves.

Kobo: Why do you think we do what we do? We're all trying to escape who we are.

Peter: Really? I didn't know.

Kobo: When I first started my own theatre, many people told me that my writing would suffer. They told me if I didn't dedicate myself completely to my craft, I wouldn't become the great writer I was supposed to be. But who is this great writer? He's a creation of others. He's not me.

Peter: So you're okay with the fact that you might never win the Nobel Prize?

Kobo: (He ponders this for a moment) Our first loyalty is to ourselves, to recognizing the demands of our own ego, and to knowing those demands are separate from us. They do not come from us

Sasha: More intellectual nonsense! Where do they come from then? My desire to be the best drives me. It allows me to shut out everything else.

Kobo: Yes, and where will you be next year when you don't have an Olympic gold medal?

Sasha: Shut up! I don't have to listen to that! I'm number one in the world. No one trains harder than me. The gold is mine to take.

Kobo: (to Peter) He doesn't know, does he?

(Peter shakes his head.)

Sasha: Know what?

Peter: The Soviet Union will boycott the 1984 Olympics. You'll miss your chance at a gold medal.

Sasha: What are you talking about? That's impossible . . . There's no way . . .

Kobo: It's true.

Sasha: Fine. If next year doesn't work, there will be the next Olympics or the next.

(Kobo and Peter shake their heads.)

Sasha: What? You're saying I'll never win an Olympic gold?

Kobo: How does it feel now? Still sure about all those sacrifices?

Sasha: Fuck you! You're not getting the Nobel either!

(Kobo looks to Peter, and Peter shakes his head "No.")

Kobo: They wouldn't have given it to me anyway. My work is too strange.

(Kobo returns to doodling on his napkin.)

Peter: Isn't it good enough that you stuck with your art regardless of what people thought, regardless of the rewards?

Sasha: I don't want to talk about it anymore.

(Kobo throws his pencil against the wall.)

Peter: But you've got your work! Kobo, you published what, fifteen or sixteen books? How many plays?

Kobo: It doesn't matter.

Peter: It has to matter! (turning to Sasha) And what about those five world championship medals? Not to mention the team titles . . .

Sasha: Without an Olympic gold, they're nothing.

Peter: I can't believe this. You guys are my role models. Sasha, you told me I couldn't have it all. Kobo, you said it was all about sacrifice.

Kobo: Do as we say, not as we do.

Peter: What's that supposed to mean?

Sasha: It means stop looking to others to find your path. There is no right path! You can do everything. Every god damned thing. You can sacrifice until you bleed. You can work and work and work only to find your own government will betray you.

Kobo: Nobody owes you anything.

Sasha: That's right, kid. The sooner you learn it the better.

Peter: So, the only loyalty is to oneself?

(Both Kobo and Sasha stare at Peter, waiting for him to finish.)

Peter: And it doesn't matter what path I take? It doesn't matter if my life looks like yours? If you had children or not? If you get married or not? Or even who you marry?

Kobo: Why are you phrasing it as if these are all questions?

Peter: And all that matters is that I stick to it, stick to my own messy life?

Sasha: Okay, now you're sounding like one of those self-help books. Can we stop before I get a soft American belly, too?

Kobo: (standing) Yes, I think our time is up here.

(Sasha stands as well. The two make as if to leave.)

Peter: Wait! Don't go! I think I'm just starting to understand.

Kobo: (to Sasha) He's worse off than we thought.

Sasha: (to Kobo) Da. He still thinks the answer lies out there.

Peter: Can you repeat the part about how we can't look for models? I think I need to hear that again. Does it mean the right path is inside us or that there is no path?

Kobo: (to Sasha) All we have is our work.

Sasha: (to Kobo) And it looks like that's all we're ever going to get.

Kobo: (to Sasha) Should we leave him?

Sasha: (to Kobo) There's really nothing we can do. Besides, look at him. He's a mess.

(Peter mumbles to himself, asking himself question after question. Scratching his head.)

Sasha: (to Kobo) We shouldn't have come.

Kobo: (to Sasha) The most important lessons can't be taught.

Sasha: (to Kobo) True.

Kobo: (to Sasha) It's sad really.

Sasha: (to Kobo) Another reason to get out of here.

(The two exit. Peter stares after them, hands out, imploring.)

Bout Seven:
Courtesy

1. *Polite behavior.*
2. *Consent or agreement in spite of fact; indulgence.*
3. *Willingness or generosity in providing something needed.*
4. *An archaic spelling of "curtsy."*

1.

Before a bout, whether it's in practice or a tournament, fencers salute each other and the referee. In the traditional salute, you stand straight, mask off, feet perpendicular, you raise your sword high in front of you, then bring it to your face and hold it there, almost kissing it. Finally, you sweep your blade to the ground with a flourish. In practice, the fencer raises his sword to his head then tips it toward his opponent and the referee. This is usually accompanied by a nod. Most fencers, but not all, look you in the eye while doing so. It is a gesture of respect, a "curtsy." It is done despite the fact that immediately after this gesture of courtesy each fencer will do everything in his or her power to stab that same opponent. Some will try to cheat. Others will argue calls with the referee, even when they know they're not right. During a bout, I've had fencers scream obscenities in my face. I've been elbowed, kicked, punched, and bowled over. And in some cases, I've done the same to my opponent. After the bout, fencers are required to return to their *en garde* lines, remove their masks, and salute as they did at the beginning. They are then required to shake hands with their un-gloved hand. If a fencer doesn't do this, he can be black carded and removed from the tournament, all record of his victories and defeats erased. At the world championships, I once saw a heated match between the Austrian, Joachim Wendt, and the Italian reigning Olympic champion, Stefano Cerioni. Cerioni won the bout, and Wendt calmly walked up to him and offered him his gloved hand to shake. Cerioni went ballistic. The entire Italian team stormed from the stands and tried to jump Wendt. The referees eventually calmed things down, but hours after, I still saw Cerioni giving Wendt the evil eye as he sliced his hand across his throat.

2.

The word "courtesy" comes from the Old French *"courteis"* and refers to genteel politeness and courtly manners, particularly in the code of courtly love. Many such courtesy books were written in order to explain the proper behavior of the courtly lover, who should, in the ideal situation, court someone else's wife. We are told that the lady involved should be of a much higher station than the lover: that she should be located at a distance, that the lover should tremble in her presence, and that he should obey her slightest wish. He should, moreover, fall sick with love, faint when he sees a lock of the lady's hair, preserve his chastity, and perform great exploits to attract the attention of the lady. . . he should spend all his wealth, employ outrageous flattery, engage in blatant hypocrisy about what he wants, and convince the lady that she can accumulate great wealth and a kind of eternal youth by granting her favors.[1]

In this sense, the "courteous" words of the lover allow him access to the walled garden of his desire. Once the lover gains access to that garden, it is over. No more courtesy. No mention of getting to know the lover on a personal level or of having a real relationship. One of the most popular of these books was *Roman de la Rose,* written by Guillaume de Lorris in 1237. It was the most widely read book in France for three centuries. Translated into many languages, it also took hold in Europe, particularly England, where it clearly influenced Chaucer.

3.

Courtesy, or polite behavior, is not always tied to genuine behavior. In fact, the goal is often the opposite, to appear polite in order to get what you want. It's all about appearances. The samurai understood this. Why else would they include it as one of the eight requirements of Bushido? If you live your life on the edge of violence, if rationality can fracture with a moment's notice, the veneer of civilization crack, it becomes essential to keep up appearances. I've always been amazed at how intensely I can fight someone on the fencing strip, how close to violence we ride, how much I can hate them, then when it's all over, after the salute and handshake, we go for a beer and laugh. In the last North American Cup, I had a great time over breakfast, chatting with what would end up being three of my most fierce opponents that day. We laughed. We talked about our kids, our jobs. Then, we walked onto the fencing strip. We saluted. The mask came down. I remember thinking he wants to kill me. I remember thinking I want to kill him. Which relationship is real? Perhaps both. Perhaps neither. Or maybe we as human beings are able to move so fluidly between the two *only* because of the elaborate rules we set up.

4.

Relationships are not much different. How quickly we move from love to hate, from happiness to anger. No wonder medieval courtiers needed an elaborate protocol to avoid problems. The Spanish writer Javier Marías talks over and over in his books of how we do nothing in a relationship except out of obligation. We oblige others, and we are obliged. The tongue, and the words that spring from it, our most potent weapons. It is the kiss of Judas as we persuade those around us to love us. What's that? You think, No, not my children. It's our children we oblige most of all. All through acts of kindness, of "love," of polite behavior, of consent or agreement in spite of fact. We indulge them, and expect in turn, that they will indulge us. Hamm expects Clov's obedience, his indulgence. And why shouldn't he? He raised him. He suffered for him, at least in his own mind. Beckett understood that, like marriages, parent/child relationships are about nothing more and nothing less than power. The courtesies we give each other are part of a complex code of obligation and obeisance.

5.

When marriage fails, when we no longer oblige our spouses or get them to oblige us, we go to therapy to learn a new set of protocols, a new form of courtesy. *I hear you and understand where you are coming from. It must be awful to feel that way.* Or, *I'd like to speak my truth now. You can't disagree with my truth. It's my truth. If you do that, you shut me down and invalidate my feelings.* We look each other in the eye as we say these things. We hold each other's hands. And we listen. We don't interrupt. We don't give in to the rising tide of anger threatening to drown us. Relationships are difficult. Love can easily twist to hate, then back again. Courtesy is what keeps us from killing each other in the meantime.

6.

We so rarely get to show our real selves. Maybe that's why I like fencing so much. It's a crucible for the real. On the strip you can't avoid being yourself. There are fencers who complain about every call. Fencers who scream after every touch as if they're trying to intimidate you by sheer volume. Fencers whose entire game is built upon deception, upon giving openings, pretending to make mistakes in order to draw your attack, so they can counter attack or parry riposte. Others whose attacks are always disguised not to look like attacks, so that you don't know they are attacking until you've already been hit. And then there are the straight up fencers, the ones who believe they disguise nothing, the ones who think they rely on technique alone to beat their opponent. I used to think I was one of these honest, upright fencers, as if that was a better way to be, as if anything is really honest. I prided myself on hitting with strength and speed. I was stupid. Nothing is ever that simple. I didn't realize until much later that fencing is all about the preparation. When an attack succeeds, it's the result of countless manipulations of timing and distance, countless feints and jukes, so that your supposedly simple and straightforward lunge is only possible because you've been manipulating your opponent all along. This is essential to the game of fencing and the game of life. It is intrinsic to the definition of courtesy. So, if all is a ruse, if every act of polite behavior is calculated deception designed to get what we want, why not drop the pretense?

7.

It turns out we need it. What I didn't mention about breakfast at the last North American Cup is that I was sitting alone in the corner of the hotel restaurant trying not to look too conspicuous before my nemesis invited me to join him and two other of my opponents that day. The guy that invited me over had been the number one veteran foil fencer in the U.S. for the last four years. I'd just threatened that title four months before when I won the first North American Cup in Dallas. You could argue that he was playing a psychological game. You could be cynical, as I've been above, and say that at a basic level he was only doing this to be seen as a good guy or to be liked. These things might be true. But it also might be more complex than that. I prefer to think that it was an act of generosity, something that is also part of the definition of courtesy and something that is inseparable from the pretense that also makes us human. His act changed my morning. It doesn't matter that he tried to kill me later in the day. It doesn't matter that he argued the final call—a call that went against him—until he was blue in the face. It doesn't matter that he later said, "There goes Grandbois with his god damned gold medal." For the moment of that morning, he kept up the veneer, real or not, and that's what makes courtesy important.

I can remember few acts in my life that appear to be genuine courtesy in the sense of "a willingness or generosity in providing something needed." My first fencing coach, Henri, sent me money to fly to my first world cup competition because he knew I didn't have it. I never asked him for it. I never even brought up the idea. Henri worked as a bagger at the local grocery at the time. The money for the trip to Paris took a huge bite out of his monthly income. Every time I think of that act, I cry. I'm crying now as I write this. Was it only because he wanted me to become a great fencer so that he would be seen as a great coach? I don't think so. It may have been part of it, but I choose to believe he genuinely wanted me to have an experience he knew would change my life. And it did.

I remember, too, when I was five years old and had pneumonia. My father was walking me through the hospital halls. I threw up, and he kneeled down before me and caught my puke in his hands. I know he may have been thinking about the mess his son was making on the hospital floor. But again, I don't think that's all of it. At the time I thought it was the most gracious act I could imagine. It also brings tears to my eyes whenever I think of it. Right or wrong, I saw it as a moment of grace, of courtesy. I saw that it wasn't about me making a mess of the hospital floor but about saving me the embarrassment of making a mess of the hospital floor. That's the way I took it at the time anyway, and that's the way I choose to take it now.

8.

We can acknowledge the pretense, accept the fact that we are complicated creatures, selfish to an extreme. We understand that we need codes of courtesy to give the appearance that we mean well, even when we often don't. And yet, at some point all that matters is the act of kindness. Fencing reminds us that beneath the salute, beneath the veneer of courtesy, lies our brutal nature. But it also reminds us that we are capable of compartmentalizing that urge toward violence and selfishness. After the bout, we take the mask off, and we salute again.

We do this so that we are able to return to the ring another time.

My wife and I have our own codes that allow us to move fluidly from love to hate in an instant. Often we don't even notice them at the time. Something as simple as making a bowl of nacho chips upon arriving home signals that this evening we will be polite to each other, we will show love to each other. Dishes left for the other to do or sitting at the computer with head phones on signal that the pretense is gone and all bets are off. A stern cast of the jaw and a glance toward the bedroom is the same as a mask coming down. You better prepare yourself. The battle is on.

What I love about returning to veteran fencing after seventeen years is that we go out of our way to be kind to one another, to talk to one another, to be civil and courteous to one another. In another life, when I was twenty-seven with the single-minded focus of making the U.S. Olympic team I took things too seriously to be courteous. And so did most of my opponents at the time. Then, it was all about bluster and brag. Another form of manipulation. Now we recognize the futility of that brag, or if not the futility of it, at least its emptiness. We invite each other to breakfast before the tournament and to dinner and beers after. We recognize that we have a responsibility to be courteous despite what might happen when the mask goes down. We understand that yes, the mask frees us, allows us to release our true selves in all their ugliness and duplicity—no wonder superheroes always wear masks—but we also understand the most important part of engaging in this dance we call human relationships is the show we make, the show that says, no, I will not let ego reign, not all the time, not here, not now. In this moment, I will be courteous not because it's the human thing to do (God! What is that?) but because we know we are capable of better. The act of courtesy is our promise to ourselves that some day we won't need the mask.

Notes

1. Robertson, D.W. Jr., "The Concept of Courtly Love as an Impediment to Understanding Medieval Texts" in *The Meaning of Courtly Love,* ed. by F.X. Newman (Albany: State University of New York Press, 1972), p. 2.

Bout Eight: Courage

I want burning.

Rumi

Courage can't exist without knowledge. A man who doesn't know or understand the potential danger when he walks into a burning building to save a child doesn't exhibit courage. A soldier who enlists dreaming of video game warfare where he rescues his friends under sniper fire doesn't exhibit courage. He can't understand until he's lived through at least one battle, even then it's only a glimmer. Wait until he returns home and has to face the PTSD. The meaningless days piled one on top of another. A woman who has one child can't exhibit courage. She doesn't yet understand the nature of the pain. Going back for the second, that's courage.

I used to be fond of Rumi's quote. I once told a close friend in all seriousness, "I want burning," as if it was something you could ask for in a store. Something you could purchase. I thought it made me cool, someone who was at once passionate and willing to risk it all. I understand Rumi was talking about a relationship with God here, a relationship beyond words, beyond ritual, beyond the known. An ecstatic relationship in which you open yourself to the divine. I know his point is that mystics get burned. The divine exists outside the human, to go there you must forego the superficial trappings of bourgeois life, the life of the family man. Like the artist, you have to live outside the narrative and sometimes, as Paul Chaat Smith reminds us, "to be outside the narrative is not to exist."[1] To be outside the narrative, that takes real courage. Or insanity. Or both.

There is no road map outside the narrative. Nowhere to go when the burning gets to be too much.

It's easy to say, "I want burning," when your life is going well. When your life fits the narrative you've written for it. I had a great job in academia. My books were getting published. My children appeared to be doing well. My marriage appeared to be doing well. The thing about fire is that it burns away appearances. To face the possibility of separation and divorce every day for three years. To have a child scream that she wants to die because the pain is too great, or that she hates you, or that she'll never forgive you because you cannot take away her pain. To stand before your child and know you can't do anything in the face of her mental illness, but to try to be there for her anyway. That's what it means to burn. To sit down with your wife and calmly discuss the terms of separation even though you both know you love each other, even though neither of you wants to separate even though neither of you could ever in your wildest dreams imagine breaking up the family. That's what it means to burn. There is no narrative for these things.

I remember around 1989 or 1990, I was fencing a direct elimination bout in Kansas or Nebraska or New Mexico—the places have all blended into one. My opponent's blade broke as he attacked. As he lunged, the broken blade penetrated my leg. Not much. More of a scratch really. A flesh wound for the Monty Python fans out there. But it bled a lot. The blood soaked my entire thigh red before they could stop the bleeding. After a short injury time out, I was ready to fence. I couldn't move my leg well, but it didn't hurt. My opponent looked pale as he returned to the strip. He couldn't muster the courage to attack me, or if he did, his attacks were feeble, and I easily parried them, then launched my own. It took more courage for my opponent to face my blood stained leg, than it did for me to fence with it. The beauty of youth is that I had no idea I could have hurt myself further.

As a veteran fencer, a fencer over fifty, it's a whole different world. Every time I go to practice. Every time I get on the strip at a tournament, I know very well what I could do to myself. My body doesn't let me forget. The tendinitis in my hand and wrist and elbow, the shooting pain in my lower back and hip, the sharp pain in my right knee, the arthritis in my left foot, remind me with each step that if I make a wrong move, I will not be the same person I was yesterday. Every morning after fencing when I rise from bed, I face the fact that I may have crippling arthritis in another ten or fifteen years. I feel it in my bones, and yet I keep fencing. Why? Why continue to fence when I know what it will do to my body? Is that courage? Stupidity? We think courage is an attribute of youth, but the young haven't the foggiest idea what the word means. You have to live a little to understand what you can lose.

A man who is not on fire is nothing.—Carl Jung

I used to think life was about achievement. I used to mark my life by the goals I'd set myself. There's something about youth that wants, no needs, to be on the move, to keep running. As a young man, I was terrified of being seen as "normal," of fitting into the narrative. And so I fenced. I excelled in medieval literature and the Old English language. I prided myself on being anachronistic. Being different. Even now I've carefully cultivated my narrative to always exist on the outside. I read international literature and books from independent publishers. Never mainstream American fiction—whatever that is. I write books for small presses, books the corporate publishing houses would scoff at because in the words of so many of my rejection slips: "We don't know how to position this." I review primarily small press books for magazines, who, in turn, primarily publish reviews of small press books. I am the champion of the fringe.

Books are dangerous. That's why they get burned. That's what sets them apart. Books, real books, not the kind that can be made into movies or video games, are the closest we can get to entering the consciousness of another, to having empathy. Real empathy. Virginia Woolf's *To the Lighthouse* kind of empathy, José Donoso's *The Obscene Bird of Night* kind of empathy, David Markson's *Wittgenstein's Mistress,* Ann Quin's *Berg,* Percival Everett's *Erasure,* William Faulkner's *As I Lay Dying*. These books cannot be made into movies, despite James Franco's megalomaniacal attempts to do so. These books use the alchemy of language and point of view to bring us inside the consciousness of another. Movies can't do that. Video games can't do that. They do plot. They do special effects. They do beautiful faces projected on a giant screen. They do these things really well. Books with a capital "B" understand the power of the word. They know that a well-crafted sentence can also burn. The right word can sear itself into flesh, the way the single word shift in point of view in Hemingway's "Hills Like White Elephants" transforms the story and therefore us—"They were all waiting *reasonably* for the train." A paragraph honed to perfection can work its way inside so deeply there's no possibility of excision. It lingers and hurts like a lost love.

What matters most is how well you walk through the fire.— Bukowski

Last night I fenced the bronze medalist from the 2004 Olympics in Athens. He visited our club in Columbus, and he kicked my ass. I asked if I could fence him again. Again, he killed me. I asked him to fence one more time. He toyed with me. I could do nothing. I would have fenced him again, but I needed to get my daughter home, who at this point was thoroughly embarrassed watching her father willingly return again and again to the seat of humiliation. I left the club exhilarated, more alive than I'd felt in a long time. No matter the fact that my elbow throbbed so much I couldn't pick up my water bottle after. My daughter laughed at me on the car ride home. "You'd fence until you dropped," she said. And she was right. It wasn't about wanting to win. Forget the tendinitis in my elbow. He was twenty years younger than me. He hadn't stopped training for seventeen years as I had. Even if I'd never stopped fencing and was magically made younger, this Olympic bronze medalist was a far better fencer than I'd ever been. It was about the dance. It was about the need to burn. It's good to get your ass kicked. Even better to get it kicked again and again no matter how hard you try.

Recently, I fenced in a local tournament in Columbus. Because it was "an open" it meant that I'd fence against men and women ranging in age from ten to seventy five. One woman there must have been seventy if she was a day. She wasn't in my pool, but she caught my attention, nonetheless. Decked out in full regalia, it was clear she'd made a significant investment in fencing. It was also clear she knew what she was doing. Her basic form was good. She understood the actions. She must have fenced for a good portion of her long life. I watched her fence her first bout. She lost five to zero. After, she shook hands with her opponent, unhooked, and calmly sat down. Ten minutes later, they called her to strip for her next bout. Again, she lost five to zero. She didn't score a touch all day. Yet, every time they called her to strip, she walked over, hooked up, saluted her opponent and donned her mask. It was only in the last instant, as her mask went down, that I spotted in the cold set of her eyes something all fencers understand. The determination to fight. It is how we recognize each other. It was not a game for her. It was not an easy way to pass the time, the way so many seniors use golf or tennis. She didn't smile. Her face held only the look of calm determination. And yet she had no hope of scoring even a touch. That's courage. That's what it means to burn in sport.

It isn't much different for the artist. I have measured out my life in rejection slips, to steal a line from Eliot. Sometimes when I tell my students that my novels have been rejected forty or fifty times, that some stories have been rejected seventy, eighty plus times, when I tell them my most recent novel took four years to write, and I've now been sending it out and having it rejected for three years, I see looks of abject horror. Then, just to kick them over the edge, I let them know that even if it does get published, it will most likely sell no more than a thousand copies. I might make a thousand dollars, if I'm lucky. Why do it? they ask, unable to fathom a process where "success" takes so long and is so difficult to measure, at least with metrics that fit the narrative, or where success may not happen at all. Why submit yourself to such a bleak process? they ask, and I tell them if they have to ask the question, they may already have their answer.

The rise of the Internet and computer software that makes independent publishing affordable has transformed the publishing landscape over the last thirty years. Many of the best books now come from small, independent presses. And yet, so few get read. Fewer still win prizes. Books from independent presses make up about two percent of the finalists in fiction for the Pulitzer, the National Book Award, and the National Book Critics Circle Award over the last thirty years. You don't believe me? Run a check. I did. Rarely, if ever, is one of those books reviewed in the major papers. There is very, very little courage in the mainstream publishing industry. And newspapers? Well, they're going the way of the dinosaurs.

Still, small presses keep emerging. They keep growing. Somehow, the books find their way into the hands of readers who press them to their lips, knowing full well the price of immolation.

What is to give light, must endure burning.—Viktor Frankl

We don't choose to burn. We don't choose when to show courage. That was my mistake in telling my friend that I wanted burning. My hubris. I had no idea what was in store for me. Had I known, I would never have said those words, never have chosen to burn. The narrative we are sold says we can control our lives. It says we can have the house with the white picket fence, marry the woman we'll love for the rest of our lives, have 2.5 children who will grow up to be happy and healthy and to do it all again. It says, play by the rules, try hard, set your mind to it, and you can have it all. It's all about positive thinking, knowing what you want, imagining it, and it will be so. But it turns out that's all an illusion designed to keep comfortable consumers. To quote Leonard Cohen, "You live your life as if it's real." When it turns out that life is about as far from that "reality" as we can imagine, that life is much messier than we've been told, many of us retreat to our addictions of choice.

Unless we don't. Unless we refuse. Allow ourselves to burn. Two years ago, I almost left my marriage. My family. Even now, two years later, it's sometimes a fight to stay in it. Some days are good. Other days, I feel as if I will break, as if I'm already broken. On those days, it's as if the next word spoken, the next sound will shatter me. My wife and I work really hard at our marriage. With three kids, and each of us in a career, it's difficult to find the time to talk. Or at least time when we're not both exhausted. When we do talk, things can go south pretty fast. It used to scare me. It used to scare me so much that I would avoid talking at any cost. I would isolate myself. Find things to do. It's easy when you're a teacher. There are always more papers to grade, lessons to plan, things to read. It's easy when you have three kids. One of them always needs your attention. It's easy when you have as many passions as I do. I can slip into fencing, writing, reading, painting, music, and never have to face the fire.

But then I started fencing again at the veteran's level. I remember walking on strip those first few tournaments and telling myself I was the best fencer in the room, that I could beat anyone. And I remember a little voice answered back. Yeah, but now any one of them can also beat you. Things are different in the veterans. It doesn't all boil down to skill, or tactics, or tenacity. It doesn't come down to who has the killer instinct, as it so often did when I was younger. In the veterans, you become painfully aware that no matter how good your technique or how strong your killer instinct, your body can fail you at any moment. You often think of the right tactical move, but your body refuses to carry it out. We are all plagued by injury, pains that affect the outcome in what often seem arbitrary ways. We, each of us, come to the strip carrying a lifetime of emotional baggage that shapes the bout. When you're young, all you want to do is win. When you're older, yes you want to win, but you also know that your opponent may have just lost his father, or that he is having trouble with one of his children. You know because you sat with him, talking about it over a bourbon the night before. You know, too, that your own worries over your children make it difficult to concentrate on this day. All of these things make winning in the veterans division seem arbitrary at best and downright capricious at worst.

It was a frightening realization to know how easy it was to lose to "lesser" fencers in the veterans. Then, almost as quickly, it wasn't. It became liberating. I realized if I didn't have to worry about losing, if it's so arbitrary, I didn't have to worry about winning. I was free to dance. Some dances are beautiful. Some brutal. But the outcome was no longer important. All that mattered was doing it. And isn't that life? Isn't that what relationships are all about?

The definition of a successful marriage is being willing to live in a mess. I don't mean a physical mess. I'm not talking about a pigsty. I'm talking about an emotional mess. I'm talking about being willing to lose, acknowledging that on a daily basis you will lose as much, or more, as you win. We have a lot of narratives of control in this country. Our entire national narrative is built on the "fact" that we are the best, that we will always be the best, that we can never lose. We are so sure that if we follow the rules, if we just do things a certain way, we will achieve success. We will be happy. We will win. But it's simply not true.

Recently, my wife and I sat out on the back deck. It was a clear night with so many stars. The kids were inside: one doing homework, the other on her cellphone, the other watching TV. It was past their bedtime, but we decided to let go of the rules for this night. We needed to talk.

"Is it time for us to separate?" I asked. "Time for us to move on?" As if there could be an answer. I didn't look at my wife but stared up into the bowl of stars.

"I don't feel like I have a husband," she said. It wasn't an attack. Her flat tone suggested just how tired we each were of the pain we continued to inflict on each other. The ways in which each had failed to support the other.

"I don't feel like I have a wife," I responded, perhaps too quickly, wanting to be sure we started the conversation on the same footing. "We seem to bring each other down."

My wife took a deep breath, and we sat in silence for what seemed like a long time. "So, what's the worst that can happen?" she asked. "We move to different houses. Shuttle the kids back and forth. Deal with the traumas that follow."

"Yep," I said, still not turning toward her. "We could even live across the street from each other. It wouldn't be that bad."

"Not really any worse than being together," she replied. And this time, she turned toward me and smiled.

I reached out for her hand. Her smile always did that to me. Took me straight back to those first few times we went out, when I'd catch her smiling at me from across the table. "I guess the world won't come to an end, either way," I said, and we both laughed.

"The kids would be okay."

"Eventually."

"Yep," she said. "Eventually."

"Look at that," I said, letting go her hand to point toward the eastern horizon. "Look how bright those two stars are. Do you suppose they're planets?"

"That one on the left is probably Venus," my wife said.

"Maybe the one on the right is Jupiter."

"Maybe."

"It's strange that they're both so bright," I said.

We sat like that for a long time, neither of us saying anything more until our youngest joined us, saying he was ready for bed. I squatted down for him to climb on my back as had become our habit, then couldn't help but point out the two planets. "Mom thinks that one's Venus and the other one's Jupiter," I said. "If you were an astronaut, which one would you rather visit?"

"I don't care," he said, sleepily. "Venus is hot, and you'd sink through the gases of Jupiter. They'd both be hard places to live."

As usual, my wife fell asleep in our son's bed, and I fell asleep in our daughter's. Only much later in the night did we find our way back to our own, but by then we were too tired to talk more. I have trouble sleeping, and so I stared out the window. I'd heard that when NASA plots a course for a mission to the moon or Mars it's not a straight line, but a series of corrections and mis-corrections, like a sailboat tacking upwind. I wondered about that jagged path. I wondered how long it would take to arrive.

Notes

1. Smith, Paul Chaat, *Everything You Know About Indians is Wrong* (Minneapolis: University of Minnesota Press, 2009), p. 51.

Bout Nine:
Honor

Honor isn't about making the right choices.
It's about dealing with the consequences.
Sophocles

A cat is penned up in a steel chamber, along with the following device (which must be secured against direct interference by the cat): in a Geiger Counter, there is a tiny bit of radioactive substance, so small, that perhaps in the course of the hour one of the atoms decays, but also, with equal probability, perhaps none.[1]

I have never spoken truly of myself.
The following pages are lies.
I have only spoken the truth.
The following pages are a testament to that truth.

Sword fighting schools date back to the twelfth century, but modern fencing begins in the fifteenth century with the Spanish school and a book by Diego de Valera. The French and Italian schools soon followed, the French taking a strategic approach while the Italians favored a more athletic approach. (The rivalry between these two schools still exists today.) It was considered a sign of cultivation to know how to fence. And of course, it was a badge of honor to take part in a duel. Between 1600 and 1780 in France alone, forty thousand French noblemen were killed in duels.[2] By the early nineteenth century more young European noblemen died from duels during the previous two hundred years than from any other cause. Dueling was tied to honor, bloodshed and violence to upholding the honor of one's family and one's name. In many ways, the duel should be considered a great advancement in civilization, as it codified the rules of violence, curtailing the more random acts: the crimes of passion and the barroom brawls. Ironically, the modern age of random violence where children can be shot in the street and even in their own schools returns us to a more barbaric time, a time without a code.

I am both alive and dead.
I am both an artist and a father.
I am a fencer and a husband.
I am a man who desires and one who has given up on desire.

In 1558, the playwright Ben Johnson killed the actor Gabriel Spenser in a duel over an unknown cause.

In 1569, Miguel de Cervantes wounded Antonio de Sigura in a duel.

In 1704, the German composer Handel was nearly killed in a duel with Johann Matheson.

In 1772, playwright Richard Brinsley Sheridan fought two duels with the same man, Captain Matthews, over a woman to whom Sheridan was secretly married. Sheridan won the first, letting the man go as he pleaded for his life. He lost the second when his own sword broke and Captain Matthews stabbed him several times.

In 1792, Lady Almeria Braddock fought what has come to be called the "petticoat duel" in London's Hyde Park when Mrs. Elphinstone made a comment about Lady Braddock's age. They fought with pistols, then swords before Mrs. El-phinstone agreed to write Lady Braddock an apology.

In 1823, the Russian writer Pushkin fought a duel with the poet Kondraty Ryleyev. Pushkin went on to fight many such duels, most famously the duel in which he was killed by French officer George d'Anthés, who was rumored to have had an affair with Pushkin's wife, Natalia.

In the American west of the nineteenth century, the duel with swords metamorphosed into the gunfight. Two men standing on opposite ends of the town, facing each other, their hands poised over their guns, trigger fingers twitching.

In 1842, President Abraham Lincoln accepted a challenge to a duel when state auditor James Shields accused Lincoln of publishing an inflammatory letter in the Springfield, Illinois newspaper. The two met for battle, which was only stopped once the seconds convinced Shields that Lincoln had never written the letter.

American President, Andrew Jackson, purportedly fought more than one hundred duels in his lifetime.

In 1897, Marcel Proust fought a pistol duel with journalist Jean Lorrain after Lorrain published a stinging review of Proust's first book. Both shots went wide of the mark and their seconds convinced them to call it a day. Proust later remarked that his biggest worry was having to rise so early. He was not a morning person.

In 1921, Benito Mussolini fought a duel with Francisco Ciccotti. The duel with swords famously lasted over an hour and a half before Mussolini wounded Ciccotti.

As barbaric as they seem to us now, duels were rooted in honor and honor is rooted in integrity in one's beliefs and actions.

To live with honor is to be authentic.
To live with honor means to betray yourself.
Codifying violence is idiotic.
Violence without rules is insane.

We pretend the violence in fencing is not real. The blades are not sharp. No one is killed or even injured (usually). Yet, walking into a national or international fencing tournament you cannot help but think you've wandered onto a battleground. Piercing screams puncture the air. Fencers charge down the strip at each other, waving swords, smashing one another on the head. At a large tournament, there is almost never a moment of silence. After scoring a hit, women arch back at the waist and let out screams that would make a pterodactyl stand up and take notice. Men rip off their masks and yell in the faces of their opponents. If you only listened to a fencing tournament you would be sure the convention hall, or gym, or ballroom ran with blood. And yet blood is rare. The violence is a pretense. It is regulated. Codified.

In the 1970's, a German barber by the name of Emil Beck[3] watched video after video of fencing bouts, studying the most efficient ways of hitting your opponent. The result was that he singlehandedly reinvented modern fencing, and in doing so, made it much more aggressive, athletic, and dangerous. In 1982, the Russian Olympic champion, Vladimir Smirnov, was killed at the world championships in Rome when the German Fencer, Matthias Behr's blade broke and pierced Smirnov's mask, running him through the eye. Several more deaths followed, almost all resulting from broken blades. I, myself, was stabbed in my right thigh by a broken blade in the late eighties and have seen two other fencers on two separate occasions run through the area between the collarbone and the neck.

The result of the sharp rise in accidents in the 1980's in international fencing was that the FIE, the governing body of fencing, regulated much stricter materials to be used in both the making of blades and in the protective uniforms. Very few serious accidents have happened since. Yet we cannot forget the origins of the sport, a sport steeped in blood.

Fencing is both violent and one of the safest of modern sports.

Soccer is non-violent and one of the most dangerous sports with fifty times the injury rate of fencing.

President Barack Obama won the Nobel Peace Prize at the same time that he increased an already bloated military budget for more war spending in Iraq and Afghanistan.[4]

You cannot simultaneously prepare for war and plan for peace.—Einstein

I don't yell as much as most fencers, and I certainly don't yell in my opponent's face, though I've experienced it too many times to count. But I do yell on occasion. I do feel the thrill of combat, of setting my body, my mind against another and trying to hit them. Yes, hit them with a sword. No matter that the tip of the sword is blunt. I'm not always comfortable with this duality. I am a pacifist by nature. When the topic of war and aggression comes up at dinner parties or among friends, I am outspoken in my disgust at even our slightest violent tendencies. If I were president, I would outlaw guns and never ever go to war. War is a last resort for a people who have lost all reason. These discussions always end the same. One of my friends will point out that my favorite pastime is violent in its roots. The point is made as if this hypocrisy should end the argument, as if by participating in a sport that re-enacts our violent past I am not allowed to criticize our violent present. This is a red herring, a sort of ad hominem attack. Vegetarians face this sort of thing all the time with comments like *What about those leather shoes?* It smacks of a sort of righteousness and political correctness that ignores the complexity of human experience, of human psychology. I am guilty of this myself as I've often labeled all people in the military as warmongers, though I have met many who are pacifists.

Like the duel, modern fencing (and much of modern sport for that matter) is simply another set of codes designed to regulate our violent tendencies, to acknowledge that we have them, but also to acknowledge that we are more than that, the sum of our parts far greater than any individual characteristic. It is an attempt to hold the duality in our hands, to accept the violence in our natures and our need to move beyond it. We celebrate the honor in sport because it allows us to live in the paradox of who we are, to make sure that violence is not the only thing in us, or at least that it's put to honorable means, at least most of the time. One could argue that the Geneva conventions represent another attempt to honor or acknowledge our capacity for both violence and peace. And in a sense that would be correct. But only in a sense. The problem in modern warfare comes when you take away the life of another who never asked to be in that war, the civilian standing by the road when the bomb goes off, or the draftee who had to sign up or face jail time, and yes, even the enlisted man who joined to serve his country but is asked instead to take part in a lie. You can write up as many rules as you'd like, but you'd be hard pressed to find honor there. War always spills beyond the edges of easily codified rules, erasing the lives of those who never gave their consent, who often never understood what their country was actually fighting for in the first place. War erases any possibility for honor because it accepts only one definition of who we are, allows for only one side of our duality to emerge.

In the first North American Cup this past year, I felt horrible for knocking my longtime friend and coach out of the tournament.

I didn't feel that horrible.

In college, my girlfriend cheated on me several times over. I hated her for that.

My next girlfriend was dating someone else during the first month we were together.

To paraphrase Hemingway, die early or life will break you. One of the ways it does so is by pointing out how difficult it is to remain honorable. When we are young, we are told: *If it feels wrong, don't do it. If it feels easy, don't do it.* Good advice. Maybe the best advice. And yet as we age how quickly we learn that sometimes easy means that it is good and right, that sometimes wrong is, if not necessary, certainly unavoidable. As we age, we come to understand that we are all inauthentic most of the time—it's a precondition of our dual natures. We want to be good, but we are not always good, so we, at least, pretend to be those times when we aren't.

I pretended for a long time that I loved my first wife because I'd married her, and I had to be good.

I have pretended my whole life that I don't desire other women because I've been in relationships, married or otherwise, and am not supposed to desire. And yet I do.

I pretended I was not in competition with my brother in our writing careers. And I am not. And I am.

I pretend to be happy when friends and colleagues publish new work. And I am. And I am not.

I pretend I don't care about winning in fencing, when of course I do. And I don't.

I have pretended to love my second wife when I haven't always been sure that I did.

I pretend to want, when what I really want is to curl up in a room and go to sleep.

I pretend to have an answer, when all I'm doing is searching.

I pretend that I am a good father even on the days when I explode at my children or stay a little longer in my office than I should.

I pretend. I pretend. I pretend.

Honor is woven from this duality. In fact, the ability to hold the duality in our hands may be the very definition of honor. It's not about integrity or authenticity as we've been led to believe, but about paradox and pretense and accepting the fact that we will, none of us, ever be wholly good or bad. This is what literature teaches us, what science teaches us. Yet, the codes of so many pop culture narratives bombard us with the notion that we are one thing or the other: good or evil, young or old, smart or dumb, beautiful or ugly. No wonder the fragile bird that flits about inside us tears its wings with the need to know who we are, which side we are on, which decision is the "right" one, which action honorable. We learn as we get older that we are all inauthentic most of the time, and yet we do our best to be authentic. We hide our violent thoughts; we repress those thoughts where we desire another; we bury the thoughts where we take what we want, thoughts where we do what we want.

The result is psychosis. The result is a culture in need of serious therapy. There is nothing honorable in being authentic if that attempt means we hide who we are. Honor is a way of being, a path toward acceptance of the beast within, toward living with that beast. Honor is the acknowledgement that we never really resolve to one state or the other. The beast is always there. Most of the big decisions are not "right" or "wrong," but both. Someone will get hurt either way. Someone will be upset. Most actions are not "easy" or "hard." They exist in an unresolved state, a state to be determined by later observation. It's the same paradox as when a champion athlete makes the impossible look easy simply because we have forgotten the ten thousand hour rule. Light is both a wave and a particle. The cat is both alive and dead.

I am a good husband, and I am the worst who has ever lived.

I am a father who loves his kids more than anything. I could walk away tomorrow and never look back.

I am an artist who dares look within. I am afraid, so very afraid.

I am a man of honor. I have no right to that claim.

Notes

1. "The Present Situation in Quantum Mechanics," by Erwin Schödinger. trans. By John D. Trimmer: https://courses.cit.cornell.edu/north/Phil_QM/Schrodinger_Cat.pdf
2. Washington State University Fencing Club Site: http://53398.orgsync.com/org/wsufencingclub/History
3. Emil Beck: http://en.wikipedia.org/wiki/Emil_Beck
4. President Obama and War Spending: http://www.washingtonpost.com/blogs/wonkblog/wp/2013/01/07/everything-chuck-hagel-needs-to-know-about-the-defense-budget-in-charts/

Bout Ten:
Passion

It is obvious that we can no more explain passion to a person who has never experienced it than we can explain light to the blind.
                                        T.S. Eliot

We fly. Not like ghosts, plucking ashes from mouths, but like birds buoyed by the blue light of wings. We skip to the back of our eyes. We shape the world perched on our fingertips. We fall to the ground like dying soldiers only to rise again, this time under machine gun fire, this time blown up by a grenade, this time under heavy artillery, this time strangled by our own hands. We rain like a swarm of bees over the wood and build our forts, our tepees, our igloos. We lift our bodies from poison-ivy scratches and torn pant tatters and lay our shadows among the trees. We melt in the afternoon sun and drip drop by drop onto the dangerous ground, then lick our dry lips and dig deep. We follow our tunnels to the center of the earth where we dream with eyes twitching of a day when we can do it all over again.

A couple weeks ago at the 2014 U.S. National Fencing Championships I was fencing in the gold medal match against a fifty-five year old fencer and two-time veteran world team member. In terms of the action, it was not a great match. His knee had given out earlier in the day and my elbow was in so much pain I could barely hold the foil. That said, you couldn't tell we were injured. Yes, there were no lightening quick phrases, no attack, parry-riposte, con-tra-riposte. Yes, my opponent fell on an attack when he put too much weight on his knee. My point is that despite our handicaps, despite the fact that we were both clearly suffering, we both fenced as hard as we could. More importantly, I smiled during the entire bout and could see my opponent's smile through his mask.

It didn't matter that we were tired. It didn't matter that we were hurting. Scratch that. The fact that we were hurting made all the difference in the world.

The word passion comes from the Latin *patere,* meaning to suffer. That usage is considered obsolete, except when you talk about the passion of Christ. When we think of passion now, we think of something like the Meriam Webster definition: "a strong feeling of enthusiasm or excitement for something or about doing something." But it's the original definition of passion that interests me.

There was something about that moment on the gold medal strip. Yes, we both had a "strong feeling of enthusiasm" about fencing. That was part of it. A small part. Bigger still was the fact that we were both suffering: the compound, running attack he made in the action after he fell from his bad knee; the way I responded in kind, striking with a combination double-advance, ballestra lunge I had no business attempting; the fact that we fought until time expired; the fact that we would have kept fighting had they let us, that much like the Black Knight in *Monty Python and the Holy Grail,* we would have continued even with both legs and both arms lopped off. These things mattered. My opponent had nothing to prove. He's a wealthy entrepreneur who travels the world. He'd already been on three U.S. fencing teams. And though I'd never made a U.S. team, I would argue I had nothing to prove either. I'd been one of the best fencers in the country twenty years before. I was a successful writer and professor with a beautiful family. And yet we were both there, risking permanent injury and guaranteeing we'd be taking plenty of Advil that night. Why?

Because when we walk into a fencing club and hear the clang of steel, when we put that mask on and smell the stench of stale sweat, when we don that glove and feel the stiff leather begin to loosen, when we pick up our weapon and sound the weight of it, when we feel the force of its arc run through our arm as we hit our opponent square in the chest, we take a step closer to that long dead definition of passion and the knowledge that if you want to feel, really feel, there's got to be a bit of suffering.

When I was younger, I thought the best part about writing was having written, but as I get older I've realized how important the writing process is to me. I used to fear sitting in my writing chair each day. I would live in terror of those moments where nothing comes, where you sit and sit and stare out the window and play with your nose, then get up and make a cup of coffee, sit down again and play with your nose. Those moments were confirmation that I didn't have what it takes to be a writer. I thought I wasn't being productive if my fingers weren't flying over the keyboard, if

I didn't churn out several pages in a few hours. Something has happened. Something has changed. I now think of the time when I'm typing as the least important, the least fruitful. Creativity happens in those moments when I thought nothing was happening at all. Nothing except sheer terror. Nothing except suffering. Those are the moments when I feel like a writer. The times when I have no idea what I'm going to do, the times when I sit on the verge of panic and despair, wondering if I'll ever write another sentence again. That's when I feel the most connected to the work of the artist.

Hemingway liked to have a plan. He preferred to stop writing at a point where he knew what was going to happen next because if he didn't, he feared the anxiety over not knowing would kill him. But it's that anxiety that drives the creative process. Let it stir the pot overnight and see what you've made by the next morning. I used to think I needed a plan in fencing, too. I would study each fencer and prepare a strategy for the bout. I'd know the first few moves I'd attempt, how to best defend myself. I don't know if we simply don't care as we get older, but as a veteran fencer I no longer study my opponents before hand. There's something too controlled, too safe about it. Instead, when the bout comes, I try to enter it without preconceptions. When my opponent attacks, I listen for his style. Is he classical or unorthodox? When I attack, I listen for the tempo of his defense. A waltz or a samba? It's true that in both writing and fencing, this ability to let go and trust the moment comes with experience. You have to have faced countless opponents to know that you will sound them out quickly, read them before they have a chance to read you, to know that the discomforting fear of the unknown is the price you pay for acting in the moment.

The blank page paralyzes many young writers. They become so afraid, they forget to listen—to themselves, to the words. They forget to live in tune with who they are. It's not easy. I forgot once that I was a fencer, and it took seventeen years to remember. I've forgotten my need for music many times. I feel as if I'm in a constant battle to listen to my writing self against the sea of voices that threaten to drown it. How many of us can say we listen well all the time? There are many reasons we may turn a deaf ear to that which is part of us, some of them valid, some born from rationalizations designed to "protect" us. The fact is the world creates a deafening amount of noise. When you sit down to write and wait and wait for those words, Facebook and Twitter will whisper in your ear. Email and the Internet will shout your name. Friends and family will call begging you to stop what you are doing. Listen to the voices and you no longer need to suffer. There is nothing harder than sitting alone with yourself, waiting for the words to come, knowing they may not come and that it's okay because grace lies in the act itself, knowing that even if they do come few people will ever read those words, and of those fewer still will care about them.

I have been called a passionate teacher; in fact, it's the word that comes up most often on twelve years of student evaluations. And each and every time I read the word, I wonder what my students think it means. I don't see myself as passionate. I'm only doing my job. I teach literature and creative writing. And I try to do it well. To the best of my ability. Do I love what I do? Yes. Do I suffer? Yes, but not in the way you might think. There's nothing worse in this world than to teach a book you love, a book you'd kill for, die for, only to have the students say, "I don't get it," "This is boring," "This is stupid." To love what you do seems like a foreign concept to most of my students. School is not about doing what you love but about figuring out what the teacher wants and parroting it back. It's about taking the courses you think you need for a "career," or more often the courses their parents think they need for a "career." University as vocational school not as a place of inquiry, a place where you discover who you are and hopefully begin to ask the questions you'll keep asking the rest of your life.

The parents are the worst. It never ceases to amaze me, perhaps because my own parents were so supportive of whatever direction I wanted to take in my life, no matter how foolhardy—well, my parents did have a difficult time accepting my fencing. But when it came to school, it was another matter: literature, physics, astronomy, biology, theatre, and creative writing. I was a major in each of these subjects at one point in my college "career," actually getting degrees in three of them: literature, creative writing, and biology. I barely passed physics, and to this day think my "passing" was a gift from the professor, who wondered how I was so misguided as to think I would become a physicist. But isn't that what college *should* be about? The exploration of who you are and your place in the world. Pushing your limits to discover what you can and can't do. Pushing so hard you fail once in a while. A journey with at least as many mistakes as successes. It should be where you find your voice. And yet, I'm not sure I've yet met a parent who didn't try to dictate—sometimes passive aggressively, sometimes through any means necessary—what their child should take in college. From the point of view of many parents, passion (in both the original sense of the word and its current meaning) is a luxury you cannot afford. I watch my students wrestle with the parental reins, some of them breaking free, others getting more tangled the more they struggle.

Is it so odd in this day and age to actually do what you love? I think so. Particularly, when what you love is something society doesn't value—like writing books, like fencing. When students come to me for advice, I tell them follow your heart. They look at me as if horns have just sprouted from my forehead and fangs flashed from my mouth. Maybe that's really what they see. After all, capitalism demands inauthenticity to thrive. It's all about turning human beings into customers and making them think they need things they don't, that they can only be happy if they could just have that thing. The messages in TV and movies are almost always to be someone else, be someone other than who you are, be a superhero, or a super cop, be a warrior or a princess, be beautiful in the same way that each two story face peering down at you from the screen is beautiful. Friendship is no longer about actually being there for someone, actually talking with them, but about how many "likes" you get on Facebook. Learning is no longer about the questions you ask but about how comfortable you feel in the classroom: no "trigger warnings" please! Vacation is not about the experience but about how many "selfies" we can take to show our friends we had an "experience." As a culture, we don't seem interested in suffering for the sake of a "questionable" activity, one that doesn't make gobs of money or instantly bring us one million "hits." We are interested in being entertained. We are interested in being "liked." We are interested in being seen. Passion means cutting the heart from the ribcage, putting it on a platter and eating it. It's hard to do that when you split open the chest and find nothing but darkness inside, or worse yet, find a video game of a beating heart or a Facebook photo, or a Twitter feed declaring to all that you have a heart, you really do.

I ask my students on the first day of class what makes a book "successful." Inevitably, one of the first hands raised mentions how much money the book makes. I then tell them that in my experience there is almost always an inverse relationship between the quality of the writing and how much money the book makes. They do not believe me. So, I give example after example. Some students agree to "think about it." Others never will. Fencing has no economic value so it can be real. Writing—at least writing that disturbs us, defamiliarizes us, challenging us to re-examine the meta-narratives we've been spoon fed, daring us to throw away our old notions and see the world anew—has no economic value so it can be real. Spend five years pouring everything you know, everything you are into a book, then another five trying to get it published by an obscure, independent press only to see that book ignored by the rest of the world. Do it again and again and maybe then you'll understand the meaning of passion.

There's not a lot of glory winning the national fencing championship in the over fifty division. And there certainly isn't any money. But I remember walking onto that final strip and saluting my opponent. When the mask came down, I remember wanting that victory more than I ever wanted anything in my life. It's not that I don't value my children, my family, my career. Of course these things matter to me. Most of the time they are all that matters. But not in that moment. And I'm sure it was the same for my opponent. When the ref called us to fence with *Allez!* I came at him with everything I had. Beat one-two, followed by a half lunge to set up the counter-riposte. He took the bait, and I slapped home a parry four. He came right back at me. And when he drilled me square in the chest, this otherwise mild-mannered entrepreneur arched back in a scream straight from the fields of Agincourt, or Maldon, or the Red Cliffs.

Most people give up on passion as they get older. Most settle into lives of compromise. This is the normal pattern as people get tired of pushing up against their limitations or the ways in which the world beats them back when they stretch too far. It's much easier, and, perhaps, in some ways wiser to accept who we are. The problem is that human beings are dynamic and not static at all, who we are is always changing, always in a state of metamorphosis, sometimes violent, demanding of us to become something new, sometimes calmly whispering that we redefine all that we are and all we've been.

Yes, the body wears down eventually, and we must listen to it. I fence in the veteran's division as an acknowledgement that I can no longer move at the speed of the elite fencers. As I write these words, I know that in two hours I'll go to the fencing club. I'll open the hatch of my Subaru and plan out how best to pull my fencing bag from the car without straining my already strained wrist. I'll enter the always too-cold salle wishing they would spend more on heating so my old joints won't take so long to feel as if they actually worked. I'll slip my orthotics into my fencing shoes and carefully wrap my fingers and wrist, knowing what a thin line keeps me from re-injuring old wounds. I'll spend double the time of the younger fencers warming up: running, stretching, doing footwork and bladework so that when I step onto the strip I don't pull anything—or at least decrease my chances of pulling anything. Most of all, I'll use that time to prepare psychologically for the pummeling I'm about to take to ego and body as I face off with four or five of the top younger fencers in the U.S. They respect me. A little. Because I make them move. A little. There is still value in pushing myself beyond what I could do yesterday, executing a parry-riposte or contra tempo better than I did before, writing a sentence that sings a little louder and clearer than the last.

> *We shall not cease from exploration*
> *And the end of all our exploring*
> *Will be to arrive where we started*
> *And know the place for the first time.*

The end of Eliot's *Four Quartets* reminds us the journey is never over. At some level, we intuit this. What is more difficult to understand is the fact that this knowledge, as Eliot also reminds us, costs "not less than everything." And that, of course, is the real reason capitalism abhors passion, offering instead cheap knock-offs from tourist shops. Not only is there no money to be made following your heart but it will take everything from you.

If it came down to a choice, few of us would make it willingly. Unfortunately, it rarely comes to that. We do it or we don't.

High above the living, there is Beethoven's Opus 131, String Quartet #14, swallowing pain, singing us toward the long sleep, blooming beneath our skin like black dahlias, reminding us what it means to be human. The baby steps onto foreign grass, the dark sea to which we retire the first time we are unloved. The bee stings in the throat. The old man watches desire wink out, night by night, like candles in the window. Smoke like ghosts of regret stealing through the thickets of our years. And here we are, waiting to hear the music, dancing blue faced and infirm with slowly burning bodies that totter toward the pounding wind while somewhere our clubfooted souls lie huddled in a corner or beneath the sheets praying for an end to the rain.

Bout Eleven:
Character

Sports do not build character. They reveal it.
                                    Heywood Broun

We are the kings of catastrophe, the queens of ineptitude. Princes and princesses of disappointment. We pile the shattered bones of our missteps on the pyre of our imperfections. Our national anthem sings of soot-black air and beaten dogs. We pledge allegiance to distant shores we will never reach and storms that drag us away from any sight of land.

At the club where I fence in Columbus, there is a woman in her early fifties who recently started fencing because two of her three children wanted to fence. She took up sabre, the fastest weapon, a weapon with no room for error. She has been a regular at the club for the past two years, fencing two to three nights a week and going to nearly every tournament. She almost always loses. She is always beautiful.

Beautiful in the way pages fluttering in the breeze are beautiful, in the way snow clinging to the railing outside the window is beautiful, in the way a bird unable to find a branch to land on is beautiful. I watch her and often wonder why she does it, fencing against kids a third her age, all of whom are faster, more agile. I know why I do it, but I, at least, have decades of fencing experience, muscle memory to rely on, even if those memories are twenty years old. She takes last place in tournament after tournament. And after, she smiles and talks of how next time she'll do better.

A gentleman at my club in his forties also took up fencing because his son wanted to do it. Fencing does not come easy. The movements are unnatural. It takes years of training for them to become normal, much less second nature. The old adage is that fencing takes one lifetime to learn the basics, another to master them. I watch this gentleman struggle through his footwork, his upper body bobbing back and forth like those clown faced punching bags. When he parries, it looks as if he is swatting at you. His attack appears more of a semi-controlled fall. He's always smiling. He tells me he loves the sport and wants to become as good as he can.

That's it, isn't it? To be as good as we can. That's the best we can hope for as we get older. I fenced my first division one national championship in 1988 when I was twenty-four years old. I came in last place. I told myself it would never happen again. I was young. I could afford that luxury. It didn't happen again. Over the next two years I worked my way from being one hundred and eighty first to placing somewhere in the fifties and sixties. A year after that, I made the top sixteen for the first time in my life. After that, many top eights or top fours. I had the time and the energy and the drive. When we're older, we're lucky to have one of those. Never all three. So we work hard and hope to be as good as we can.

We, none of us, expected to fail. And yet we do. Every day. We fail despite our best efforts. We measure ourselves against that failure. Maybe this time we won't lose quite as badly. Maybe this time we'll have made our opponents work at least a little bit for their touches. Maybe this time we wont' be quite so sore the next morning. Maybe we won't have the usual aches and pains. Maybe we'll be able to get out of bed. To walk down stairs. To sit. Without pain.

A flick attack in fencing involves cranking the arm and throwing the weapon forward with a whip so that the blade bends and the point hits the opponent's back. It used to be my bread and butter. It takes a lot of arm strength. I remember the first time I tried flicking when I came back to fencing at forty-eight. I slapped my opponent across the shoulder. I apologized. I tried again, and apologized again. I couldn't generate the torque required to bend the blade enough. No matter. Two years into my return to fencing and I have "Tennis Elbow." It's difficult enough to attack with a straight arm now, much less attempt a "flick." If I did, the pain shooting up my arm would force me to drop my foil. In veteran's fencing, practice doesn't always lead to improvement. It often makes you worse. Wisdom is to know your limitations and work within them.

Twenty years ago, I was famous for running my opponents down. My nickname was "the rhino." When I first tried to fence with my old run and gun style, I nearly tripped and fell. My hip went out on me. My knees gave way. My body told me its limitations. I didn't listen much the first year, but I've learned to listen since. My game is different than it was twenty years ago. For the first time in my fencing career, I use the clock. I take my time and instead of attacking, I offer false openings designed to draw my opponent out so I can capitalize on my hand, which thankfully remains quick. My legs are another matter.

We drag our wings through dark, cloudless nights, the moon flailing our corpse. We open our mouths to song and hear nothing but a dry rasp. We lift our feet in dance but find them tied down by the low sound of distant bells. Time stops, and we fall backward, teetering on the edge of our regrets. We pull our coats tighter at the throat amidst the ash falling from our hair. We are the fathers of the big flop, the masters of miscarriage. We are the butchers of botchery, and the disciples of disaster. We court failure as if there were nothing else in the world we'd rather be doing.

I started and restarted this essay four times before I got it "right." I still don't know if I have it "right." The previous essay also took several attempts before I found a mode that worked, or at least felt like it worked. The curse of age is that you know enough to know you are wrong far more often than you are right. The old Japanese proverb: *Fall down seven times. Stand up eight.* To know, too, that no matter how much you work at it, no matter how much effort you put in, you may never get it "right." It is also a blessing because at some point you free yourself to be *as good as you can.*

When I wrote my first novel, I was a relatively young thirty-eight and oh so lucky. I didn't know what I was doing. The fool's blessing. I sat down every day at my computer and simply wrote. I completed the first draft in six months, then spent the next six months revising it. I probably put the novel through three drafts total. I sent the novel out to a round of publishers and the first email response I received was an acceptance. I didn't know enough to know how rare it all was. My second novel took four and a half years to write. I have over forty different drafts saved on my computer. The novel was rejected forty-five times before it found a home. My third novel took five years to write, had a similar amount of drafts and after seventy plus rejections is still looking for a home. Writing doesn't get easier. When we write, we think we are "approaching truth," but the older you get, the more you realize how elusive that "truth" is. Even if you find it, you understand how difficult it is to express. I remember the summer I began writing that third novel. I wrote to page sixty, then stopped, trashed it and started again. I repeated this process at least four or five times until I found the voice and the form necessary for the story I wanted, no needed, to tell. Even when I found the voice and form, writing wasn't necessarily easier. I just knew what I had to do. But knowing and doing are sometimes as different as a boy and his father. Whether it gets published or not, I consider that novel my finest work, and my biggest failure.

Several years ago at a library in Sacramento, while sitting on a panel and talking about writing, someone asked how I defined "success" as a writer. I'd never thought about it before and so wasn't ready for the question, and was even less prepared for the answer. At the time, I only had two books out. The first had won many awards, been seriously reviewed, was under contract to be made into a movie, and had sold several thousand copies. The second had sold maybe four hundred copies. I told the audience that the second was a much bigger success to me, though it would probably be deemed a failure by every such metric we use in America. I told them there were two reasons why: the first was that even though many more people had read my first book, I'd received a few personal emails from people regarding my second book saying how it had changed their lives. In other words, I marked success not by how many readers I had but by how deeply a few readers received it. Finally, I was more pleased with the writing in my second book than in my first. In other words, I'd met my own standard in that book, not the standards of somebody else. That book was called *The Arsenic Lobster: A Hybrid Memoir,* and is a prequel of sorts to this one.

Lord deliver us from the ugly hands of "success." Take us, instead, down the road of failure in the trunk of a dead car. We beseech you to protect us from paths with a pot of gold at the end, roads that appear too easy. Let us wake to the blank page each and every day and not be sure how to fill it. Let us enter our daily tournament knowing each and every person there can beat us. We ask that you pluck out our eyes so that our black sockets can roll back into heaven. Grant us scorched earth that our dying weeds might grow. Only then can we know strength. Only then can we understand character.

As in writing and fencing, the longer I live, the less I realize I understand. The more I realize how much of my life is defined by failure, how failure defines me. You can't go through life without making mistakes, and I've made more than my share. A ruined first marriage. A nearly ruined second. I have failed to keep up with so many, many friends. Failed to listen to myself at key points in my life. And yet I would argue that these failures are not even the important ones. The ones we see clearly, the ones we remember right away, those shape us, but less so than we think. It's the thousand little failures we ignore each day that really make us who we are, and nowhere is that more clear than in parenting.

As a father with two teenage girls and a headstrong ten-year-old boy, I've almost completely given up. Children have no lack of compunction in letting you know when you've fallen short of the mark. The teen who reminds you of the promise you failed to keep or the conversation you failed to hear or the fact that you failed to understand her need for a break from piano practice or homework. The child who reminds you that you failed to see when he needed help or when he didn't need help, when he wanted your love and when he didn't. To give your teen a kiss or a hug when they don't want it can sting worse than a bad book review.

But parenting is only one part of a very long day. I fail to play with my dogs enough. I fail to pay the bills on time, to keep the house clean, to maintain the yard and clean the garage, to keep up the deck and the exterior paint. I fail to prepare enough for the classes I teach and spend enough time on the papers I grade. I fail to get the cars in for a tune up or an oil change or a tire rotation or to check the battery. I fail to love my wife enough. I fail to sleep at night so I can be rested for my failure the next day. Failure to be *as good as I can be*.

And yet, I wouldn't have it any other way. That's not quite true. Rather, I know there is no other way. In fencing, I will always lose more bouts than I will win, at least if I'm pushing myself. In parenting, I know if my kids love me all the time, something is wrong. I haven't done my job. I've tried too hard to be their friend. In writing, if my book is reviewed in the *New York Times* (Don't worry, my books will never be reviewed in the *New York Times*), I know I've failed to express the deepest part of who I am, my vision of the world. For good or ill, our lives are measured by our mistakes.

We are the rulers of ruin. We are the tyrants of tragedy. We court calamity at every turn. We wake to upheaval and work through confusion. Mayhem, havoc, pandemonium are our middle names. We live for discouragement. We pray to be washed up, washed out, let down and defeated. We settle for setback and know in our bones that we'll spend far more time in the anticlimax than the climax. We are born thinking we are conquerors but we die knowing life is a rout.

So why do I fence? Why return to a sport in which I have no hope of being as good as I once was, a sport where I'll be reminded of my failures, my shortcomings every day? It is the great lesson of getting old: to accept that we are ninety percent failure in blood and bone, that we take last place more often than not, that we are all desperately trying to be as good as we can be. The body is the first to remind us when at thirty our backs start to go out from time to time and our arms aren't quite as strong as they used to be. At forty, our legs don't quite carry us with the same grace. By the time you reach fifty, if you don't understand that you've failed at nearly everything, you've either got your head in the sand or you never set your bar high enough in the first place. Failure is necessary for growth.

That lesson can be the hardest of our lives: to know that we live on a receding shoreline and that soon everything will abandon us. Grace lies in looking out from that shore, knowing no one will come, but standing there anyway. We live in an age of instant gratification. In all my years of coaching, I've seen hundreds of young students come to fencing thinking they want to be Aragorn or Luke Skywalker, then quitting a month later when they realize they can't be instantly good at it. They lack the necessary character. As a professor, I get email after email from students trying to convince me I should let them into my classes: "I have a passion for the short story." "I have a passion for poetry." "A passion for words." "A passion for writing." They love the word passion, mistaking that for character. And yet, when I tell them to come on the first day and see if a spot opens up, none of them show. How quickly their passion fades when things are not certain, when life is not handed to them. Much of the fault lies in youth. Character is born from pain and sacrifice. Discipline and time. Above all, time. Age understands the way in which character is tindered in work, ignited by failure.

Our culture celebrates winning above all else. We call our sports figures heroes, as if somehow they've sacrificed for us. Maybe they have. Maybe the ten thousand hours they sacrificed practicing, trying to get better, wasn't really for them, but for us, so that we would have a model of perfection and grace. Maybe. But I'll take the people who don't make the six and seven figure salaries, the people who don't make the news. I'll take the woman who doesn't win a bout but keeps getting up and donning her mask anyway. I'll take the old man I used to fence with in Denver, who was always the first to arrive at the club and the last to leave. He was dying of cancer, and though his legs could barely move, he was the only one to never take a break. "Do you want to fence?" he would say with a smile. And how could you refuse. His hand was still quick. He knew what it meant to fence *as good as you can*. He lived it. And for a moment, when you fenced with him, you lived it, too. Despite youth. Despite the false promise of what lay ahead. You hoped that someday you would understand enough to make a parry riposte the way he could. Simple. Without thought to the past or the future. Without a worry about who you were or who you would become.

We are the memory of winter. We are the dying bird sputtering over the ground. We are an open mouth without sound, an abandoned car at the bottom of a ravine. We are the last drops of rain to fill the muddy tracks. We are the long night when the rain doesn't stop. We understand our lot. Still, we return again and again. And we won't stop. Not ever.

Bout Twelve:
Justice

Justice to the left of you. Justice to the right. Speak when you are spoken to, but don't pretend you're right.

YES

It will come when you least expect, the day you're walking in the woods and your death unfolds before you like a script from *The Walking Dead* or maybe Pitt's *World War Z,* or, if you've been particularly bad, Austen's *Pride and Prejudice and Zombies.*

Trees flash from ash to cinder to nothing. Justice, this arid wasteland, this desert you cross twice, first with nothing to say, later with nothing worth saying because *nothing comes from nothing,* the only thing you remember from Shakespeare a lifetime ago

The twenty-first century American landscape is crawling with zombies, the monster *sine qua non.* If the entertainment industry is a reflection of our culture's secret fears and desires, then surely something must be said about the plethora of walking dead among us. You can't shake a stick without hitting a zombie. You can't take a step without falling into a post-apocalyptic wasteland complete with razed cities, vast uninhabitable asphalt deserts, and the inevitable highways rendered un-passable by abandoned cars.

I'm sure the cultural theorists are hard at work on deconstructing these avatars of the American unconscious as opposed to actually opening a real book, but they'll most likely spend years scribbling indecipherable notes and quoting from Derrida and Foucault to make sure we all know how smart they are, so let me save everyone the trouble. The wasted landscape and walking dead brains are manifestations of our unconscious fears. We've externalized our deepest nightmares, and it turns out that nightmare is the realization that we have become empty carcasses, bags of flesh walking about, rotting in the sun. We've forgotten who we are or even what it means to be human, and so we wander the scorched earth in search of brains.

Every culture gets the heroes it deserves, and we deserve the zombie hunters: those men and women who think nothing of shooting their former friends and relatives in the head, blowing their brains out. We cheer when they find new and improved ways to scatter those brains, even when by the end of an episode they are covered in them. It's as if we want the zombie hunters to put us out of our misery, as if we can't bear living with the memory of what we once were.

Justice is seeing yourself as you are. Your follies. Your mistakes. Your insignificance. Your emptiness. That's supposed to be one of the benefits of growing old. And the curse. However, instead of looking inward at that emptiness and grappling with its consequences, we project it on the big screen and shoot it in the head in our desperate attempt to rid ourselves of what we fear we've become. That's the thing about the zombie apocalypse. There's always more of them. No matter how many you shoot, they keep coming, until you look them square in the eye without fear, without a gun, a crossbow, a poker, or ice pick. But zombies are slow. And dead. Or undead. I've never been quite sure. They shuffle around not knowing who they are or where they're going, attracted by sound, or movement, or smell, or whatever it is that attracts zombies. They shouldn't be that scary. They shouldn't overwhelm us. Overpower us. We should be able to escape. And yet we don't. Time and time again, they corner us in some alley sans exits, or in the woods backed up against a cliff, or on the top floor of a building without a fire escape. Eventually, they overwhelm us with their sheer numbers. It should not be so, and we are left to wonder why.

Because it's easier to be entertained than to think. Easier to recite the Pledge of Allegiance than to question your government's motives when they start yet another war. Easier to say *We are not like them,* than to say *We are more like them than we care to admit.* To put yourself in the place of your enemy is the greatest act of empathy. How much easier it is to say we are the shining beacon of hope in a world that is evil than to admit to the evil within. Welcome to the heart of darkness. As a culture, we've taken the easy way out time and time again. We Americans. We've chosen the military industrial complex, the prison industrial complex, the Hollywood industrial complex, Monsanto and drones. We accept the fact that our presidential debates are no longer debates but prepackaged sales pitches, that political discourse is no longer discourse. We accept the insanity of our broken schools, our ridiculous healthcare, and the fact that we may very possibly be the most violent society on the planet all because it's so much easier to stay home, heat up some popcorn and watch the zombies on television. And because we as a culture refuse to face the post-apocalyptic

landscape within, the zombie hunters mete out justice one
bashed in, bullet ridden, ice picked, crossbow bolted head
at a time.

Memory is a three tiered, three layer,
velvet cake designed to make you forget
the justice of the bones crunching beneath
your tired feet as you walk through the dark wood,
the final night of your   The hole filled with
echoes of names of those you want to love.

Toss in another and listen, hope it
floats back on honeyed breath, maybe speaks your
own name. Maybe calls you back from the grave
yawning wide, another pit you're too tired
to fill though the rank breath rises to meet
you. But where your head should be there's

nothing, a hole you wriggle your finger
in, one in which your brains slowly seep out.

   As of the writing of this essay, I'm fifty. Time for me
to look within. I understand why the zombie hunters are
necessary. It's pretty goddamned frightening. I thought I'd
looked within once before—seven years ago when I wrote
my first memoir, *The Arsenic Lobster*. That book argued that

life was a fight. The only thing that counted was living on the edge, as if you had a giant arsenic lobster hanging over your head. Writing. Fencing. Flamenco. Do it all. Keep achieving. Don't stop. Keep writing books, winning medals, learning new forms of guitar. If you stop, you die. If you stop, you turn into a zombie. At one point in that memoir, I state that I'm afraid to look within: *What if when you look within there is nothing but a strip mall?* Of course that strip mall was another manifestation of the post-apocalyptic wasteland. In running from what I feared, I became that very thing.

I still believe that life is a fight, but not the kind of fight I'd originally thought. Not the kind of fight where success is measured by the number of books and medals you have, the number of skills you've attained. That fight smacks too much of the need for glory, for self-gratification. It's an easy trap to fall into, especially in an America dominated by *Just do it!,* a culture obsessed with self-gratification, a culture where children are pushed to become superstars the moment they enter little league sports, where taking dance or soccer or gymnastics is not enough. You've got to devote your life to a game, to a pastime, to an activity that used to be about being with others. Now it's about proving you're the best, proving how you can crush those others.

I've lived most of my life that way. Pushing myself. Never looking back. Rarely looking at those around me. The medals have come. The books arrived. I gave them a quick glance, then focused my attention on the next one. I thought I was fighting the forces of a culture determined to entertain itself to death. And there's truth in that. Maybe. Maybe there's truth. But it's not the whole story. Not by a long shot. The truer story is that I was running, not fighting, driven by fear of what lay within, my attention always in the future, focused on that next big thing. Maybe I'm slow. Maybe some of you figured this out a long time ago. Each of us takes the journey at our own speed. I didn't know that society wasn't the problem, the real zombie wasn't waiting for me out there on the abandoned highway or the flattened cityscape, but inside in the form of an ego that wants and wants (always more brains to eat!) because wanting is a form of avoidance, because wanting keeps you from looking in the mirror.

If you had told me justice was one long

goodbye, I would have smiled to be polite,
then climbed in my car and driven as far
away as possible. But you didn't
say a word. And now the doors are all locked,
the windows rolled, and no matter how hard
I try, I cannot stop this fucking thing.

And now there's nothing left to do but keep
driving so we don't have to look out the

window. Keep reciting the words 'til we
forget all's a pretty fiction. A dream.

I began this memoir two years ago with the idea that I would chronicle my return to the sport of fencing and the reasons why someone might return to a sport when they are older, a sport in which they can't possibly be as good as they once were. I wanted to talk about why it was important to endure pain, to be exhausted, to face failure. I thought it also meant I would be facing myself, my marriage. I was wrong. Okay, I learned a few things. Pushing the body to the point where it breaks forces you to discover humility. I learned a little more about real courage, real character. I came to understand what failure means. Except, always, always, there was the goal of making the U.S. Veteran World Championship team. Always, there was the thought that I would "fix" my marriage, or if not, that I could at least, escape it. Always there was an eye cast to the future. The lessons about courtesy, mercy, and honesty held truth but conveniently allowed me to cover up a bigger lie. I was trying to redeem my past, to make the U.S. team I'd been denied twenty years before, to redeem a marriage in which I'd spent the better part of my life. The stench of ego was still there. The goal of the world championship team provided the smoke I needed so I wouldn't have to look at myself, my life, my family. Most of all, by continuing to move, to train, to fight, I wouldn't have to acknowledge the zombie within.

Zombies are scary because maybe, just maybe, they're real. Maybe we are nothing. Maybe nothing about us is significant. Maybe we just shuffle mindlessly through this life until someone puts us out of our misery. Medals, books, guitars—all these things allow us to pretend otherwise, to attempt to give some sort of significance to our lives. Making the world championship team twenty years after I failed to make it was, for me, the last great attempt to create that false sense of significance.

Well, in 2014 I made it. I won all three of the North American Cups in my age bracket. They sent me my official sweats, my stars and stripes mask and bag. I was in the club. I made up a schedule and trained harder than ever before. No matter that I'd be spending two months living out of a Rhode Island hotel with my daughter as she received treatment for her OCD. Have fencing bag will travel! We spent each day at the hospital as she underwent six hours of intensive treatment, then at night, I took off to fence at the nearby club. At first, it felt good. I told myself I needed the break, the release from the tension. And the truth was, my daughter needed a break from me. She begged me to get out of the hotel room. So, I left her alone to read, to deal with her disorder while I fenced. I needed to take care of myself, so I could take care of my daughter. *Please make sure the mask is fastened securely on your own face before helping someone in the seat next to you.* Then, ever so slowly, I realized the world championships meant nothing to me. What

I thought had been my dream, was a mere sham. I'd been running for so long, running from myself, I forgot what it meant to sit still in a room with myself, with my daughter, with my family. To sit still and be uncomfortable. It wasn't about the fact that we'd amassed a substantial debt due to a year's worth of medical bills. It wasn't about the fact that I missed too much work to take off a week to travel to Hungary for the world championships. Okay, these were factors, but they weren't the deciding factor. The real reason I knew I would never make the trip to Hungary for the World Championships was because for the first time in as long as I can remember, maybe the first time in my life, I knew my place was home.

So, after accepting my berth on the U.S. World Veteran team, I declined. I withdrew from the world championships. It was one of the hardest decisions I've had to make, and it was the easiest decision I've had to make. At age fifty, I'd finally grown up. I let go of my "dream." I let go of the allure of that "other" life. Because of course the life we live is never the one we want. The self we inhabit is never the true self. That person is always around the corner, waiting to be discovered in some exotic locale, say, for example, in Debrecen, Hungary where you will face the greatest fencers in history: the Germans and Italians, French, Chinese, and Russians. I accepted the fact that I may not have a "true" self, that I may be a zombie after all, or at least that there is a zombie lurking somewhere inside me, and that's okay.

Of course, that's what it's all about in the end. Acceptance. Not fighting.

Accepting who we are in the moment. Accepting what our moment is. My moment was to be at home, to let go of my dream. There is a saying, often attributed to the Buddha, though no one seems to know for sure: "In the end only three things matter: how much you loved, how gently you lived, and how gracefully you let go of things not meant for you." The trick, of course, lies in recognizing what is not meant for you when the ego is screaming it's all yours. So, I let go, gracefully. Well, sort of. As graceful as we can be as human beings. After watching my daughter's suffering for the better part of the last two years, after seeing her bravery as she faced her own fears in an intensive out patient clinic, letting go gracefully was the least I could do. I needed to be with my family. Nothing else mattered. And maybe that's the other thing we can learn from the zombie apocalypse. Be there for those around you. Help them. Open to them. Let go gracefully of what you think you need, of who you think you are. Because you are nothing. The zombies know it. They'll feast on your brains without hesitation. And though others might celebrate your "achievements," though others might need them because they give us all hope, keep us distracted, keep us entertained, they will not keep the zombies away.

It's the same in marriage. I'm not going to sit here and say that my wife and I turned it around, that we have a wonderful marriage now, that we nurture and love each other. The zombies would smell the lie the same way they can sniff out brains. Marriage is a fight. Every day. A fight with the other. A fight with the self, with the need to be right, the need to win. Why did Belmonte get back in the ring? Because he knew everything but failure is a fiction. Marriage is the ultimate ring. The Thunderdome: *Two enter, one leaves.* My wife and I walk into the ring each day knowing we could separate just as easily as we could stay together, that we could hate each other as easily as love. It is a choice. Justice means working through that choice every day, understanding that's the price of living in a committed relationship. The moment you take it for granted is the moment the zombies attack.

Many of you are probably thinking it was obvious. You would have never needed to take the long and painful journey I had to take.

And so I drop my crumbs, unspool my thread.
Ode to pain. Ode to passion. Honesty.
Humility. Exhaustion. Character.
Ode to Courtesy. Loyalty. Mercy.
Ode to Courage. And Honor. And Justice.
Prithee, nuncle, be contented! 'Tis a naughty night to swim in.

And now there's nothing left to do but lick
our wounds in the middle of the night, the

middle of this wat'ry cave, this blinking
abyss—and dream of the winter when we'll
leave this world. The snow falling like seed we
throw into our future in hope that those
who come after will accept all that we
couldn't.

    I began this book with a fight, and that's where it ends.
The zombies are always there. And it's so easy to fall prey
to them. To let down your guard. To give in and sleep. But
there is sleep and there is sleep. And some sleep is necessary. Sometimes we learn more in failure than we ever do in
success. The medal around our neck shines, but that shining distracts, pulls us ever further away from ourselves and
all we hold dear. The battle isn't about winning. It's about
accepting that loss is part of the game. It's nothing new.
It just took me a while to figure out. I don't think I'm the
only one. I think humans have been moving backwards for
eons. A hundred years ago, we understood far more than
we do now. A thousand years ago, more still. We are like
the child who ages backwards. I'm not talking about factual
knowledge. I'm not talking science. I'm talking about the
knowledge of what it means to live, to be part of this earth,
to be part of the lives of those around us.

    At one point in the *Bhagavad-Gita,* Arjuna and Krishna
stand together in their war chariot preparing for battle. Arjuna is worried, and Krishna explains to him he has nothing to fear:

Your words are wise, Arjuna, but your sorrow is for nothing.
The true wise mourn neither for the living nor the dead.
There never was a time when I did not exist, nor you, nor any
of these kings,

Nor is there any future in which we shall cease to be . . .
Realize that pleasure and pain, gain and loss, victory
And defeat, are all the same: then go into battle.

There is no difference between winning and losing. The greatest warriors accept this. Wouldn't it be something to see that in a Nike commercial? No difference between winning and losing. What if they talked about failure and pain, exhaustion and humility on a Gatorade label? They are as important as honor and courage. As important as achieving your goal. As important as winning. Maybe more so. Sometimes we learn more from giving up, from letting go, than from holding on to victory at all costs. I'm not saying you need to become one of the zombies, only that real justice comes from the courage to look within and acknowledge that the zombie is there. It's inside of you. It's part of you. Listen for its groan when it rises up through your throat. Know when you need to spend a little time roaming the back woods. Just don't eat any brains.

2014 U.S. WORLD VETERAN 50-59 MEN'S FOIL TEAM
ON THE DAY OF THE NATIONAL CHAMPIONSHIPS
(BEFORE THE AUTHOR-2ND FROM LEFT-WITHDREW)

Acknowledgements

I'd like to thank the following journals in which some of these essays first appeared:

Bending Genre: part of "Honesty" appeared here as "Shooting Dinosaurs"
Broad Street: "Pain"
DIAGRAM: "Mercy"
Essay Daily: "Character" appeared here as "Ode to Failure: On the Essential Art of Failing." It also appears in the anthology, *How We Speak to One Another: An Essay Daily Reader* (Coffee House, 2016.)
The Los Angeles Review: "Courage"
Mount Hope: "Passion"
Normal School, The: "Exhaustion"
North Dakota Quarterly: "Honor"—This essay was also chosen as a "Notable Essay" in *Best American Essays,* 2017
Prairie Schooner: "Courtesy"
Under the Gum Tree: "Humility"
Word Riot: "Loyalty"

Thanks to Jane Delury, Betsy Johnson Miller, and Margot Singer for their generosity and insight into early drafts of this book.

Special thanks to Renee D'aoust, whose *Body of a Dancer* provided inspiration, and to Margot Singer, who stopped in my office one morning and told me: "You should write a memoir about returning to fencing after twenty years."

I'd also like to thank my brother, Dan, whose brilliance in "The Effort" inspired my own essay, "Exhaustion."

Thanks to Denison University and the generosity of its DURF grant for giving me the time and resources to write this book.

Finally, thank you to my teammates on the U.S. Veteran Men's Foil team and to all the wonderful people with whom I've fenced and trained. You get it.

PETER GRANDBOIS is the author of eight previous books, the most recent of which is *This House That* (Brighthorse Books, 2017). His poems, stories, and essays have appeared in over one hundred journals. His plays have been performed in St. Louis, Columbus, Los Angeles, and New York. He is a senior editor at Boulevard magazine and teaches at Denison University in Ohio. You can find him at www.petergrandbois.com.

CPSIA information can be obtained
at www.ICGtesting.com
Printed in the USA
BVHW03s2359190618
519509BV00001B/8/P

9 781947 980525